SURVIVORS

## Dedication

To all the children whose lives were changed by the Halifax Explosion of 1917.

# SURVIVORS

## CHILDREN OF THE HALIFAX EXPLOSION

JANET F. KITZ

NIMBUS
PUBLISHING LTD

PHOTO COPYRIGHT
IN CANADA 1917
BY W. G. MACLAUGHLAN
HALIFAX N.S.

Nimbus Publishing Limited        Design: Kathy Kaulbach, Halifax
P.O. Box 9301, Station A         Copy Editor: Susan Williams
Halifax, NS  B3K 5N5             Printed & bound by Best Gagné
(902) 455-4286                   Book Manufacturers Limited

Canadian Cataloguing in Publication Data
Kitz, Janet F., 1930-
The survivors
ISBN 1-55109-034-1

1. Halifax (N.S.)—History—Explosion, 1917—Juvenile literature.
* I. Title.
FC2346.33.K5& 1992      j971.6'225      C92-098649-8
F1039.5.H17K57 1992

Photos credits: Maritime Command Museum pgs. 4, 52, 54, 57 (bottom), 67, 102, 104,
107 (bottom); Maritime Museum of the Atlantic pgs. 9 (top), 39, 46, 69, 88 (right),
129, 130 (bottom), 131 (top), 133 (top); Public Archives of N.S. pgs. 12 (inset), 16
(left), 25, 32, 44 (inset), 70, 72, 74, 84, 90, 92, 95, 96, 97, 98, 125; Cheryl Castle pg.
15; City of Toronto Archives pg. 85; Marjorie Davidson pgs. 117, 126; Merita Dobson
pg. 18; Noble Driscoll pgs. 2, 109; Dorothy (Swetnam) Hare pg. 42; Ronald Herold
pg. 41; Jean Hunter pg.16 (right); Anne (Swindells) Ihasz pgs. 13, 21 (top), 82, 83;
Evelyn (Johnson) Lawrence pg. 133 (bottom); Helen (Upham) Matheson pgs. 71, 73,
114, 131 (bottom); James Pattison pgs. 14, 36, 80, 81; Beth (Thompson) Smith pgs.
1, 31 (top), 112; Barbara (Orr) Thompson pg. 100; Sharon Ward (maps) pgs. 3, 33;

# Contents

## Acknowledgements

Many survivors of the Halifax explosion that took place on December 6, 1917, can tell interesting, exciting, and sometimes tragic accounts of that event. Their own experiences are often more dramatic and incredible than the adventures of fictional characters in books.

As I worked on research for my previous book, *Shattered City,* I became very interested, not only in the explosion related experiences of survivors, but in the lives of the Richmond children in general. Gradually I found out more about the schools they attended, the work they did there, their interests and hobbies, the clothes they wore. James Pattison still has his complete set of grade seven textbooks and his homework notebooks. Other homework books were among the material in mortuary bags.

Over the years, I have talked with many groups of children in schools and in the Maritime Museum of the Atlantic. They were interested in the dramatic stories of the explosion, but also in the differences in their own lives and those of the children of seventy-five years ago. I decided to mingle the two. Some of the characters in this book also appeared in *Shattered City,* but in a different context. Since the previous book was published, my research has concentrated on the school children of the time of the explosion. *The Survivors* is the result.

When I came to select stories for this book from my taped interviews with survivors, I was faced with a difficult choice. All of their accounts gave a picture of what it was like to live in Halifax in 1917, and how the explosion changed their lives.

The people whose adventures I have related here have all helped by searching their memories for detail, and by lending me photographs, school books, and letters. I am very grateful to them, and to others too. Merita Dobson, Jean Hunter and Marjorie Davidson, with their vivid recollections of living in Richmond and of Richmond School, gave me valuable background information and photographs. Beth (Thompson) Smith, Anne (Swindells) Ihasz, and Helen (Upham) Matheson, the daughters of survivors, were all generous with photographs. Anne also lent me family treasures. Gary Castle has been responsible for reproducing much of the photographic material, sometimes repeating the process to achieve better results.

To all of them, and to every survivor of the explosion who has shared precious memories with me, I wish to say, "Thank you."

# Chapter 1

# December 1917

It was the fifth of December, 1917. Winter was just beginning in Halifax, Nova Scotia, a busy port on the east coast of Canada, but no real snow had fallen yet. There had been a few flurries, just enough to make the children start thinking about tobogganing on some of the hills in the city. In part of the north end known as Richmond, there was plenty of open space with a variety of hills—steep ones like Fort Needham for the adventurous and gentler ones on the fields for beginners.

The Orr family lived in a big, white house on the corner of Kenny and Albert Streets in Richmond. Just below the Orrs' house was Mulgrave Park, a slope leading down to the harbour. The children would be out there on their sleds or toboggans the minute there was enough snow. Only Barbara, the oldest of the six Orr children, was not longing for snow as she had found another interest for the winter. She had learned to skate and loved it. Barbara was waiting for ice to form on the nearby pond so that she could try out her new skates and boots.

December 5 was a Wednesday, and although the Orr children should have been in school, they were all at home. Barbara's younger brother, Archie, had caught whooping cough in late November, and the children were in quarantine for ten days. That meant they were not supposed to mix with other children, for fear they

Barbara Orr

*Facing page:* Barrington Street in Halifax, 1917.

Noble Driscoll

would pass on the infection. However, none of the others had become ill and they were hoping to go back to school the following week. Only Archie would have to stay home until his cough disappeared.

Fourteen-year-old Barbara was very good at entertaining her younger brothers and sisters at home. They played games together, and she read to the two little ones. She knew how to cook and bake too, and was a great help to her mother. Barbara had been kept busy the whole time they were out of school.

Not far from the Orrs, across Mulgrave Park and along Barrington Street, lived the Driscoll family. Their back windows looked out on the Narrows, the channel which connected Halifax Harbour to Bedford Basin. There were fourteen children in the Driscoll family, nine boys and five girls, but two were already married and away from home. Noble Driscoll was a year younger than Barbara Orr, but was in the same classroom at school and was a friend of Barbara's brother, Ian. Noble and Ian shared an interest in ships and had become expert at recognizing the different types that daily passed through the Narrows.

Since World War I had broken out in 1914, Halifax had become the most important port in Canada, as it lay on the east coast, closest to Europe. The city was much busier and more crowded than before. Soldiers could be seen everywhere. Large numbers were stationed there to protect the port in case of enemy attack. Others

were in training to become fighting troops and still
more were waiting for ships to carry them across the
Atlantic to the war. In April, 1917, over fifteen thousand
troops had left Halifax by sea.

Sailors' uniforms were a common sight too, and not
only Canadian ones. There were plenty of British and
American naval men and a few from the other countries
that were fighting on the same side as Canada. Neutral
cargo ships came into port, but their sailors were not
allowed to land, in case there might be spies among
them. Even though enemy ships were kept as far away

Convoys of ships crossed
the Atlantic from Halifax to
Britain and France carrying
troops, supplies and
ammunition.

as possible, German submarines had been sinking ships uncomfortably close to the Nova Scotia coastline.

So many of the ships were being lost that, earlier in 1917, the convoy system was started. A group of thirty or more ships would gather together in Bedford Basin, where it was sheltered and safe. When they were ready to leave, they would pass, one after the other, through the Narrows into the main harbour. There they would meet an escort of heavily armed destroyers and fast gunboats. The Driscolls had a wonderful view of the convoys coming through the Narrows. Noble would shout, "A convoy is coming!" as he urged everyone to run to the windows or join him in the backyard. At first the other members of the family hurried to watch, but they soon lost their enthusiasm, and Noble would stand by himself, eager to notice every detail so he could describe everything to his classmates who were not

Troopships, often seen in Halifax harbour, were "Dazzle" painted to confuse enemy submarines.

lucky enough to live so close to the harbour.

Noble's friend, Ian Orr, had his own favourite spots for watching the convoys. From the high ground in Richmond he could see the ships making preparation for departure. He also had a good view from the window of his own livingroom, where he could refer to his collection of books about ships. He had been given a pair of binoculars for his birthday and was now able to spot details that he had missed before. "You would be very useful to a German spy, Ian," his father said,

laughing. "You must know more about these convoys than any of them." The new "Dazzle" patterns, much more striking than the usual camouflage painted on the ships to confuse submariners and prevent them from getting an easy target, looked spectacular with all their strange shapes. Ian had painted his own models with "Dazzle" designs.

James Pattison

Ian and Noble were not the only boys in Richmond who were keen on ships. Their friend, James Pattison, was constantly drawing diagrams of vessels he had seen, and his homework book contained lots of different examples. The Pattisons lived further along Barrington Street, not far from the Dry Dock. Thirteen-year-old James nearly always made a detour round that way to see what ship was being repaired. Gordon, James' older brother, was more interested in military battles and uniforms.

During the first week of December, 1917, the boys were busy watching a convoy that was being made ready to leave. Two of the merchant ships that would be part of it were being loaded at the Richmond piers. Both would carry wheat brought by rail from the prairies and one would also take horses as part of its cargo. Some of these animals would pull carts filled with supplies for the battlefield and others would be ridden by cavalry soldiers from mounted regiments.

Ian Orr was actually not too sorry to be missing school because of his quarantine. It gave him more time to watch the activity in the Basin. The famous British cruiser, H.M.S. *Highflyer*, stood by to escort the convoy. Wherever its sailors went, they received a heroes' welcome. The *Highflyer*'s sinking of a large German cruiser not so very far out at sea had been widely reported in the local newspapers. Ian, Noble and James would boast to their friends if they managed to talk to one of the sailors.

From the high ground near his house, Noble could see a neutral ship from Norway, the *Imo*, lying a little apart from the other ships in the convoy. It was waiting to leave for New York to pick up its cargo. Neutral ships like the *Imo* could cross the ocean without fear of enemy attack but, as an obvious sign to other ships, BELGIAN RELIEF was painted in large black letters on its side. Belgium had suffered very badly in the war and was urgently in need of food, clothing and other necessities. Noble had noticed that there seemed to be a lot of movement on the ship when he left for school that morning. He expected that it would be gone by the

An anti-submarine net was stretched across the harbour to protect the ships in port.

time he came home. The *Imo* was a big ship, and he was disappointed because he had wanted to see it sail past his house.

On December 5, the *Imo* had been given permission to depart, but the boat bringing the coal supplies it needed as fuel for the voyage had arrived late. By the time the coal was loaded into the bunkers, the *Imo* would not be able to make its way through the harbour and out to the open sea before dark. Large nets had been stretched across the harbour in two places to bar German submarines. A gate in the nets was opened at certain times of day, but always closed after dark when a submarine might slip through and do terrible damage to the ships anchored inside. The *Imo* would have to wait until morning.

Noble was surprised to see the ship still at anchor when he came home from school. Then he noticed the little coal boat just leaving the *Imo*'s side. "That would be the problem," he said to his brother. "I bet it held them up. We'll see it leave after all. I expect they'll want to get away first thing in the morning."

One of the places Noble, Ian and James liked to visit on weekends or holidays was Point Pleasant Park. From a point overlooking the sea, they could watch the naval duty boat open or close the gate in the submarine net. They could also see the examination boat stationed by McNab's Island. Often there was a ship anchored nearby, waiting for permission to enter the harbour. Ian

The *Mont Blanc* had to wait at the examination anchorage off McNab's Island near the entrance to the busy harbour.

The *Mont Blanc* carried a very dangerous cargo.

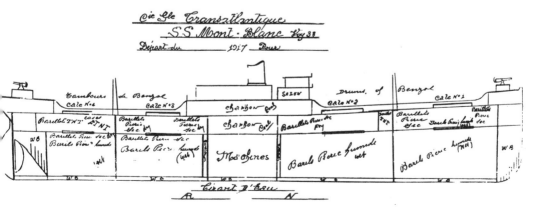

sometimes went to the park with his family and would sit for hours with his binoculars, while the others went walking or playing on the beach, imagining that he was helping to run Halifax Harbour. He would hide his binoculars if he saw a uniformed man approaching. After his father's remarks, he did not want to be arrested as a spy.

On the evening of December 5, a French ship, the *Mont Blanc*, arrived at the examination anchorage off McNab's Island. Its crew was thankful to have reached shelter. The Halifax naval authorities were also relieved. They had been expecting this vessel as they had received a special wireless message from New York about it. The report said that the *Mont Blanc* could not manage enough speed for the convoy that was being organized in New York harbour so it had been ordered to proceed alone to Halifax, where the next convoy to leave would be made up of slower ships. The *Mont Blanc* might not be fast enough to keep up even with them, as it was very heavily loaded. Special orders would be given to its captain in Halifax. If it held up the other ships, the *Mont Blanc* would be ordered to leave the convoy and cross the Atlantic without an escort.

The cargo the *Mont Blanc* carried, a mixture of explosives and a type of gasoline, was so dangerous that special care had been taken when it was loaded in New York. One spark could set off an explosion, and the dockworkers all wore cloth covering over their metal studded boots when they worked on the ship. They put up thick wooden partitions to keep the T.N.T. and picric acid apart, before carrying the boxes of explosives into the holds. Then they carefully placed the barrels of benzine on the decks.

On the way to Halifax a severe winter storm struck, and slowed the *Mont Blanc* down. Finally it arrived at the mouth of the harbour and stopped at the examination anchorage. The officer in charge inspected the ship's papers and cargo list, and greeted the local pilot who had just come on board from a ship that was leaving port. Regulations required large vessels to have a pilot to guide them safely through the harbour. The *Mont Blanc* was not allowed to go into the main harbour, but not because of its cargo. The gates in the submarine nets had already been drawn shut for the night. The *Mont Blanc* would have to anchor and wait until next morning.

# Chapter 2

# Life in Richmond

Richmond, the most northerly part of Halifax, was where many of the industries and big works were found in 1917. Because of that, the railway was very important. It linked the port with the rest of Canada and the United States. The lines ran right along the harbour. Many local men, like Noble Driscoll's father, worked on the railway. He was car inspector at the Richmond Yards, not far from his home on Barrington Street.

Barbara Orr's father was a partner in the Richmond Printing Company, also on Barrington Street. Inside its large building, made of granite blocks, both men and women worked the large, heavy printing presses. Barbara's grandfather and two uncles were partners there as well.

James Pattison's father was the mechanical superintendent at the Acadia Sugar Refinery, the tallest building in the North End. It stood at the edge of the harbour, near the Graving Dock, the dry dock where ships could be held for repair.

Another boy whose father worked at the refinery was Wilbert Swindells, usually just called Bill. Bill lived very close to Noble Driscoll. His father was a cooper, making the wooden barrels that were needed for storing and shipping the sugar products.

All of these men lived close enough to their work to walk there. Few families owned a car. Workers could be seen on the streets at practically any hour of the day or night walking to work or back home. The railway and

*Facing page:* The railway lines ran alongside the harbour, past the Narrows, and around Bedford Basin.

*Inset:* The Acadia Sugar Refinery, where James Pattison's father was mechanical superintendent, and Bill Swindells' father worked as a cooper.

Bill Swindells

James Pattison (back row, far right) and his friends diving very close to where the *Mont Blanc* blew up.

*Inset:* The Pattison boys swimming near the Dartmouth shore, unconcerned with the ships in the background.

many of the factories operated twenty-four hours a day.

Most people lived in wooden houses with backyards. Noble's family, like many who lived in Richmond, kept a cow for milk. Bill Swindells' mother raised hens for eggs and the occasional chicken dinner. There was plenty of open space, and, in summer, the children picked baskets of blueberries not far from home. It was like living in the country.

Evelyn Johnson

Catholic families sent their children to St Joseph's School on Kaye Street. It was a girls' school, and practically all of the teachers were nuns. The Catholic boys' school had burned down, but a new one, the Alexander McKay, was being built opposite St Joseph's and was almost ready. Meanwhile, the girls and their teachers were attending St Joseph's in the morning, and the boys, with their own teachers, used the building in the afternoon.

Evelyn Johnson was in grade six at St Joseph's. She was musical and took extra piano lessons before school in the morning. That meant getting up early, but she enjoyed the work and practised hard. Evelyn's father was a stock porter at the Richmond yards, looking after the animals that were being shipped by rail.

In open ground between Barrington and Veith Streets stood the Protestant Orphanage, with its own hospital and one-room school. Miss Dexter, the only teacher, taught sixty-seven students from grades one to four. Most were children who lived in the orphanage because they had no one to take care of them. Some might go

Dorothy Swetnam

Evelyn Johnson was in
grade six at St. Joseph's
School for Catholic girls.

The Pattison, Driscoll, and
Orr children attended
Richmond School.

home again after their fathers came out of the army. A
few children, like Dorothy and Carmen Swetnam,
attended school there because it was nearby. They lived
on East Young Street, close to Kaye Street Methodist
Church where their father was minister, and were in
grades one and two. But in early December they were
both in quarantine like the Orr children, and could not
go to school because Dorothy had whooping cough.

Most of the Protestant children in Richmond, like
the Pattisons, the Orrs, the Driscolls, and Bill Swindells,
attended Richmond School on Roome Street. Mr
Huggins was principal. He lived further out of the city
in Rockingham, but travelled in every day by train and
walked up the hill from Richmond Station. His ten-
year-old daughter Merle came with him, even though
there was a school closer to her home. She was in grade
five with Barbara Orr's younger brother and James
Pattison's sister. Barbara was in grade eight, Noble, Ian

and James in grade seven. All four were taught by Merle's father.

The three oldest Upham children, whose father was the yard master at Richmond Station, were in the lower grades. Their house on Rector Street was close by. Ellen Upham had just started school and was in grade one. Archie was in grade two, and Millicent in grade three. There were also two little ones, still at home.

Because the factories and railways were so busy due to the war, many new families had moved to Richmond. An additional wing had been added to the school but already it was hardly big enough and two more classrooms were being built. Children started school when they were six and usually left when they were fifteen, either to begin work or go to high school. Special permission was given to leave at fourteen, if a child had to go to work to help the family, and had passed grade seven examinations.

The school was attended by 421 students in seven classrooms. Because there had been ninety-four children in grade one in 1916, the class was split in two. In all schools it was considered normal to have sixty or more pupils in one room. Richmond was not unusual. Grades five and six were taught by one teacher, and that made seventy-two pupils altogether. Mr Huggins instructed the top group, grades seven, eight and nine. He had sixty students altogether, but only nine in grade nine. That was just as well, because they had to study

Latest fashions, from the Eaton's catalogue, worn by younger children.

high school subjects, like Latin, algebra and physics.

On these December mornings, quite a number of students were absent from school. Many of the children had caught whooping cough like Barbara's brother.

It was very unusual to have perfect attendance in any of the grades at any time of year. Sometimes, in grade one, half the children would be off sick at one time. There were many colds, as well as mumps, measles, chickenpox, and whooping cough, not to mention the more serious infections like scarlet fever and diphtheria.

Miss Campbell's grades five and six class with seventy-two pupils. This picture is very old, so some of the faces are faded.

Either of these might keep a student in hospital or in bed at home for weeks. A whole term or even more could be missed. The medicines that were available did not help very much.

Sometimes a large sign would appear on the door of the house with the name of one of the infectious diseases written in clear letters. DIPTHERIA it might read. The house had been "placarded," warning people to keep away as someone inside had been stricken with this dreaded infection. Diptheria was especially dangerous for children, and there was no inoculation against it.

Even pets were not supposed to enter the sick room of someone with a serious infectious disease. Only the person taking care of the patient was allowed inside. When the sick person was either cured or had been taken to hospital, the house was disinfected. So were all the clothes and toys. Books had to be burned in case they spread the infection later, so the best loved ones were kept elsewhere.

One of the most dreaded infectious diseases was smallpox. Babies were supposed to be vaccinated against it, but some parents did not believe that vaccination was safe and would not allow it to be done.

Every week, the school nurse would come and examine any child who seemed to need attention. This service, begun in 1915, helped to improve the health of many children. The school doctor examined every student once a year and also gave eye tests. Often a problem, like weak vision or infected tonsils, was discovered and treated. A school dentist visited as well. Because outside doctors and dentists charged fees, those who treated the children at school were of special help to parents who could not afford extra medical bills.

Beginning December 3, Richmond School pupils were able to stay in bed for an extra half hour. That day the winter timetable began. School started at half past nine, so that the children could leave home in daylight during the short days of winter.

Everyone had homework to do.

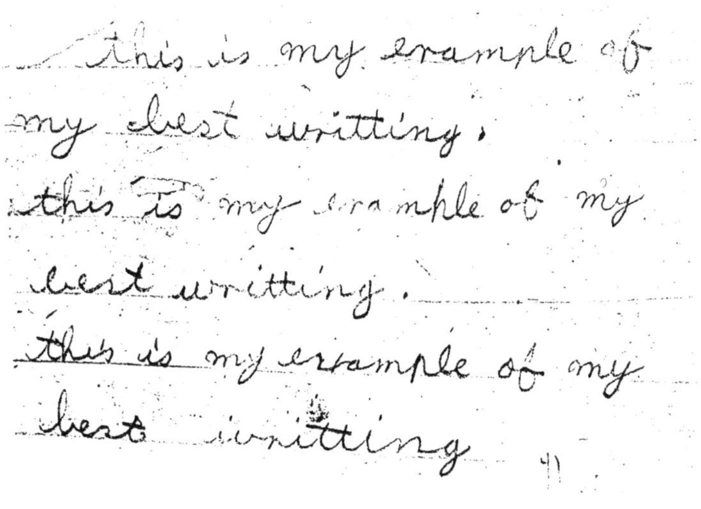

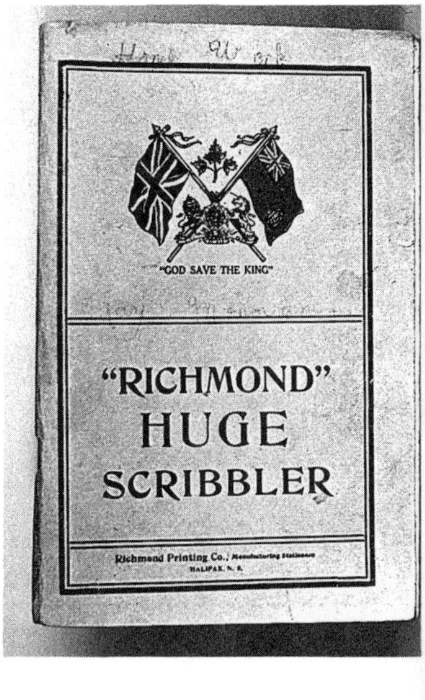

As there were so many children in every classroom, discipline had to be quite strict, and there was little

this is my example of my best writting; this is my example of my best writting. this is my example of my best writting

"GOD SAVE THE KING"

"RICHMOND" HUGE SCRIBBLER

Richmond Printing Co., Manufacturing Stationers
HALIFAX, N.S.

individual attention. One group would be given written work to do while the other was being instructed by the teacher. Some lessons, like arithmetic tables, were chanted aloud by the whole group. Even those who did not know the answers too well enjoyed reciting because the ones who had learned their tables thoroughly said them loudly and drowned out the others.

Slates and chalk or hard slate pencils were often used, especially in the younger grades. They could be easily erased and used over and over again. Archie Upham hated the noise the slate pencil made if it skidded over the slate. It set his teeth on edge. He looked forward to being in grade three like Millicent, who now wrote with

Millicent Upham

Items in the pocket of a boy from Richmond School.

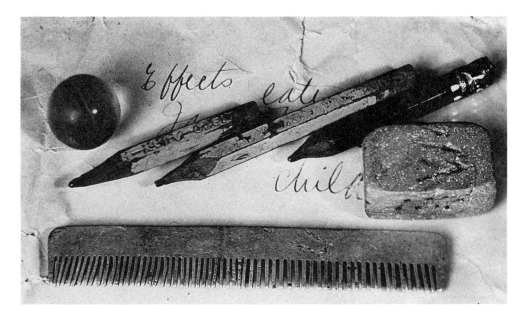

Eaton's 1917 catalogue advertised school supplies. When they were new the nibs wrote more smoothly.

**GOOD VALUE IN PEN POINTS**

Special Package Containing 4 DOZ. ASSORTED PENS Like Illustration

| | | |
|---|---|---|
| 34-174. Per package of 48 pens... | | 15c |
| 34-175. Waverley Pen Nibs, 1½ dozen in box. Per box... | | 12c |
| 34-176. Pickwick Pen Nibs, 1½ dozen in box. Per box... | | 12c |
| 34-177. Ball-pointed Nibs. Per dozen... | | 10c |
| 34-178. Spencerian Nibs, No. 1. 1 dozen... | | 10c |
| SOLD ONLY BY THE GROSS | | |
| 34-179. EATON'S School Pens, No. 292. Per gross... | | 25c |
| 34-180. EATON'S "J" Pens. Per gross... | | 30c |

a pencil on a notebook with lined paper. She was very neat and enjoyed copying out a sentence all the way down a page to show off her best handwriting.

Bill Swindells had started grade six, where some writing had to be done with pen and ink. Each desk had an inkwell filled with dark blue ink that grew thicker and dirtier the longer it lasted. Bill found it very difficult to get just the right pressure so that the pen nib did not split or scratch. Barbara Orr was used to the school pens, and the pages of her ink writing book looked immaculate. Unlike some of the students, who always had inky fingers, she never got too much ink on her pen and made blots. James Pattison wrote well too, and when he reached the end of a sentence, he enjoyed carefully laying the blotting paper exactly on top of his work while the ink was still wet to try to make a perfect mirror image on the blotting paper.

Noble Driscoll sat behind Barbara Orr in class. Barbara had bright red hair, usually braided into two

## PENHOLDERS

| | | |
|---|---|---|
| 34-133. **Pneumatic Easy-Writing Penholders** with rubber grip. Easy to hold. 6½ inches long. Each... | | 5c |
| 34-134. **Swell Penholders**, nickel grip, 6½ inches long. 4 FOR... | | 10c |
| 34-135. **Penholders**, suitable for school, home or office. 2 dozen for... | | 10c |

pigtails, tied with ribbon. One day, during a lesson with a visiting teacher, Noble gave in to temptation and gently dipped one of Barbara's pigtails in the inkwell. She turned her head and the ink flew in all directions. The teacher told Noble to stand up. "Did you do that?" she demanded. Noble admitted that he was responsible. "Go straight to Mr Huggins," she said. Noble went, trembling a little, but was lucky to find the principal in a kindly mood. He scolded Noble but did not give him the strap, as Noble had expected.

Everyone looked forward to Friday afternoons which were devoted to special projects. The discipline was much less strict then too. All sorts of things were brought to school. There were stamp collections, knitting, sewing, models, and some students even brought a friend or a cousin who was visiting from out of town. Young people were encouraged to have a hobby, as they needed something interesting to keep them busy at home, especially during the long winter evenings when they could not be outdoors.

Barbara Orr was very good at sewing and handcrafts and also played the piano. James Pattison was fond of drawing and painting, especially boats. Often he drew from memory the destroyers he had seen in the harbour. Most of the boys could draw ships, and pretty accurately too. Ian Orr and Noble Driscoll used to sit together, pointing out each other's mistakes and putting in little changes, perhaps adding a funnel or an extra gun.

Boys who were twelve years old or more were urged by Mr Huggins to join the Junior Cadet Corps. After school he trained them in drill and physical fitness, signalling and rifle exercises. Backwards and forwards they marched, carrying their long, heavy rifles, stamping their feet in step in their stout boots. In summer, the best marksmen among them went across to McNab's Island to aim at targets there. Winter practice took place in an indoor gallery with full-sized rifles that were very big for the boys and quite difficult to handle. The boys found all this very exciting.

James Pattison and his brother, Gordon, were both cadets. It was a proud day when they were taken to Clayton's huge store in the city centre to be fitted with uniforms. They had to be kept very clean and well pressed but their mother helped them with that. Their father, who had been a soldier, encouraged the boys to be smart and practise their drill.

Noble had joined the cadets but met with a problem. He was very small for his age. On one of his first parades, a senior cadet officer was present. He watched for a while and then drew Mr Huggins aside. Although he spoke quietly, Noble heard him say, "I know that these rifles are on the large side for junior cadets, but I do think that cadets should not be as much smaller than their guns as that one is." He pointed to Noble, whose career as a cadet was ended soon afterwards.

When there were parades on special occasions in

Halifax, the cadets were always on duty, either standing at attention or marching behind the band. Both James and Gordon Pattison had been part of an honour guard at a state funeral a year earlier and had stood at attention for a very long time while the procession passed. Although it was cold and they began to feel stiff, they were honoured to play an important part in the ceremony. The Richmond School Cadet Corps was known for its smartness and training, as well as skill in shooting. In 1915, 625 teams from all over the British Empire took part in the National Rifle Association Competition. The Richmond Cadets won two prizes. Al Driscoll, Noble's older brother, was a member of the team and one of its best shots. Only one other Canadian team

James and Gordon Pattison were both cadets.

won a prize. The boys spent a great deal of time perfecting their skills.

Girls could not be cadets but they had other interests, often connected with the church. The Richmond students nearly all attended one of the nearby churches, either Grove Presbyterian, Kaye Street Methodist or St Mark's Anglican. Catholic children attended St. Joseph's Church, very near their school. Barbara, James, Noble, Millicent and Archie Upham, and Bill Swindells all attended Grove Presbyterian with their families. Every Sunday, dressed in their best clothes that were not worn to school, they attended church in the morning and Sunday School in the afternoon. On Sundays, the girls wore hats, even in summer, and the boys had suits, with short trousers or knee breeches for the younger ones, and jackets to match. Long trousers were not worn until the top grades.

There was no movie theatre in Richmond. The closest ones were on or near Gottingen Street. The Empire Theatre was on Jacob Street. In November, 1917, it advertised, THEATRE COZY AND WARM. NEW HEATING INSTALLED. This was a real attraction since many of the buildings were cold and uninviting.

The Empire Theatre was the favourite place of many of the older Richmond children. Noble Driscoll loved to go there. The trolley fare was five cents, but he would often decide to walk, saving the money for a candy bar. The Empire, for the special price of five cents at a Saturday matinée, featured film stars like Mary Pickford,

Douglas Fairbanks or Charlie Chaplin. Organ music played along with the film, as there was no sound track to supply voices. The music would grow faster and faster or it would be happy or sad and slow, changing to suit the action on the screen. The children liked the organist too. One episode of a serial was also shown each week. It always stopped at a thrilling place and continued the following Saturday afternoon. If Noble unavoidably missed a week, there was usually a chance to catch up on the story during recess, when the talk was often about the Saturday adventures in serials like *The Lightning Raiders*. In November of 1917, it was advertised that *Rebecca of Sunnybrook Farm* was coming shortly to the Orpheus Theatre on Granville Street. Mary Pickford would play the heroine. The boys were not terribly impressed, but the girls begged their mothers to take them or allow them to go, even though it was up town and more expensive.

The children also kept themselves busy with clubs and activities in the church halls. In summer there was always a picnic with races and games. Early in December of 1917, the children were looking forward to the church Christmas concerts and parties. Some of them, especially the good singers, were taking part in the entertainments. The Orr children were missing all of these preparations, and for that reason Barbara was anxious to be out of quarantine. She wanted to take part in the rehearsals for plays and choirs that had already begun. It was an exciting time of year.

# Chapter 3

# Morning, December 6,1917

The morning of Thursday, December 6 was bright and clear; the few patches of mist on the harbour were hardly enough to be noticeable.

At about twenty to nine, Barbara Orr had just waved goodbye to her father who had left to walk the short distance to his job at the Printing Works. Now Barbara was standing at the big bay window in the dining room, idly looking out at the harbour. She had a fine view of all the ships that entered or left Bedford Basin. As she watched, Barbara noticed one ship coming up the Narrows. Then another appeared from the opposite direction, heading towards the Basin. They seemed to be getting a bit too close to each other.

"Ian, come and see what's going on!" Barbara called out to her brother, the ship specialist. They both watched with great interest what was happening in the harbour below them. Soon their excited exclamations brought their mother. The ships, by this time, were very close together.

"They are trying to run into each other!" cried Barbara. "There is plenty of room."

Now, even without the help of Ian's binoculars, they could read BELGIAN RELIEF on the side of the bigger of the two ships. They knew that meant its cargo would be goods for Belgium. At school during a class on current affairs, they had heard of the terrible things happening there because of the war. "That's a neutral ship," Ian said. "Otherwise it would have to be in a convoy." It

*Facing page:* The start of an ordinary day in Halifax, December 6, 1917.

was the one that was coming out of the Basin, heading for the open sea. Now they could even read its short name, *Imo*.

Just then, the smaller ship, the one heading for Bedford Basin, made a swing over towards the middle of the channel. Perhaps it was trying to get out of the way. If it was, the change of course only made things worse. The Belgian Relief ship's nose struck it on the side, near the front, and almost at once the neutral vessel pulled back. Smoke began to trickle out of the wedge-shaped hole it had made in the other ship's bow.

"That's an ammunition boat," Ian commented.

"Which one?"

"The smaller one that was hit," he answered patiently.

George's Island at the entrance to Halifax Harbour.

"What do you mean, an ammunition boat?"

The knowledgeable Ian, busy with his binoculars, explained, "That's the kind of boat that carries bullets and gunpowder and things like that. I can see barrels on the deck too. It's called the *Mont Blanc.*"

"Will it explode?" Barbara was a bit anxious.

Mrs Orr, who had joined them by this time, said calmly, "Oh, I don't think so." There were lots of men on the docks and other ships round about. The relief ship that had struck it was still nearby, showing no signs of moving off in a hurry. No one seemed worried, and the sailors would know if there was any danger, she thought.

Ian Orr

Barbara and Ian and their sister, who had also come into the room, wanted to go down to the shore to have a better look. The fire was growing bigger by the minute, and they could see other people hurrying down the hill. "Put on your coats and boots then," said their mother, "and don't go too close."

Just as they left the house, Barbara saw the lifeboats leave the burning ship and head for the Dartmouth shore on the far side of the harbour. The men in the boats were rowing as hard as they could.

Barbara had a friend who lived nearby. She too was off school because her brother had whooping cough, and Barbara thought she would run over to her house and see if she would like to come and watch the fire. "You go on if you like," she said to the others. "We'll join you in a minute or two."

Barbara Orr

Ian and his sister hurried straight down the hill, while Barbara cut across Mulgrave Park. She did not run. Her attention was taken up with watching the fire rising higher and higher, and she kept slowing down to turn round and look. The burning ship was slowly coming closer to Pier 6, not so very far away. She could hear the tremendous roar of the fire. It now drowned out every other sound. There were no more voices, no shouts, only the deafening thunder that rose into the air.

The fire had become spectacular. It was a calm, still day, with no wind. The column of black smoke went straight up into the clear, pale blue winter sky. Balls of fire rolled through it and burst, with showers of sparks. Barbara stood still in the middle of the field, spell-bound, her friend forgotten. But it was strange—all of a sudden everything went silent.

A huge column of smoke mounted into the clear sky.

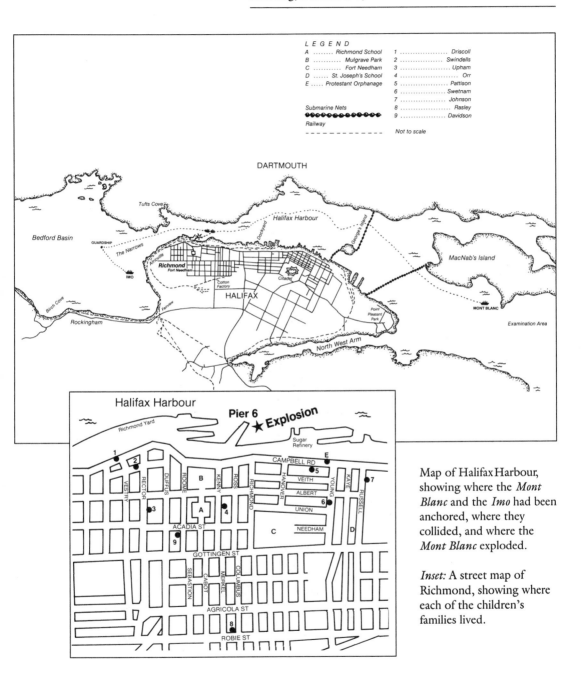

LEGEND

| | | | |
|---|---|---|---|
| A | ........ Richmond School | 1 .................. Driscoll |
| B | ........... Mulgrave Park | 2 .................. Swindells |
| C | ........... Fort Needham | 3 .................. Upham |
| D | ...... St. Joseph's School | 4 .................. Orr |
| E | ..... Protestant Orphanage | 5 .................. Pattison |
| | | 6 .................. Swetnam |
| | | 7 .................. Johnson |
| Submarine Nets | | 8 .................. Rasley |
| | | 9 .................. Davidson |

Railway

Not to scale

Map of Halifax Harbour, showing where the *Mont Blanc* and the *Imo* had been anchored, where they collided, and where the *Mont Blanc* exploded.

*Inset:* A street map of Richmond, showing where each of the children's families lived.

Noble Driscoll

At about half past eight that morning, Noble Driscoll was out in the back garden, playing with his little brother, Gordon. They were still not used to the new timetable, and had got up at their usual time; now they had half an hour to fill in.

After three years of war, the boys were used to seeing ships of all kinds pass their backyard. They knew that some of them carried munitions but were sure that the naval authorities were keeping everything safe. Also, they had heard of the terrible losses that Canadian soldiers had suffered in the war in Europe and very much wanted them to win. The armies needed guns and ammunition to beat the enemy. At school they often talked about the war, especially in Noble's class, where Mr Huggins taught them current affairs.

That morning their attention was attracted by the ships' whistle blasts coming from the harbour. They ran over to where they could have a better look and were just in time to see the bigger ship strike the smaller one. As they watched, smoke began to come from the gash, only a little at first but quickly growing thicker and thicker. Noble was excited. "I'm going to get Pop," he said to Gordon, who did not seem to care quite so much. When Noble rushed in, Mr Driscoll was sitting beside the window, eating his breakfast before leaving for work. He listened calmly to Noble's description of the collision.

"I'll just finish my breakfast first," he told his son,

"and then get my things together for work. I'll come
and see what's up as soon as I've done that."

Noble was a bit disappointed at this calm reception
of his exciting news but he did not argue. When he went
outside again, Gordon had gone. Noble thought he
must have seen one of his pals and left for school. He
had better be going too, he thought. However, he
decided to take a slight detour to see how the boats
were doing. One was really on fire now. A huge mountain
of smoke rose from it, and it was moving closer to the
shore. He saw two small boats, crammed with men,
heading quickly away from the ship; they were almost at
the Dartmouth shore by this time. They must be
escaping from the fire, he thought. Noble wasted no
more time. He wanted a better look at what was going
on. He ran as fast as he could along the street until he
came to Creighton's store. Cam, the owner's son, was
standing outside the shop, watching the excitement. Al,
Noble's brother, drove a horse and wagon delivering
groceries for this big store, and Noble was well known
to the people there.

"Don't go any closer, Nob," Cam warned, knowing
full well where the boy was heading. "There's bullets
exploding, and you might get one in your leg." Noble
could barely hear Cam over the noise of the fire, but he
stopped where he was. Maybe he had gone close enough.
Just at that moment an unnatural silence fell.

James and Gordon Pattison

The morning of December 6 saw the usual rush and bustle in the Pattison household as the boys prepared for school. Catherine, their sister, had a nasty cold, and Mrs Pattison had said that she should stay in bed. The boys' schoolbags had been packed the evening before, after they finished their homework. Alan did not have quite so much homework, but now that James and Gordon were in the upper grades, they had a lot.

Several days earlier, James and Gordon had gone with their parents to the jeweller's shop to pick out watches. Gordon had chosen a wrist watch and James a pocket one. That morning James had lent his to his father whose own watch had been sent for repair. James missed digging into his pocket, pulling out his fine watch and reminding people of the time, even when it was not really necessary. But this morning it was Gordon who looked at his wristwatch and announced that it was almost time they left for school.

Their mother insisted that they dress warmly, as it was a cold morning, even though the sun seemed to be coming out. They put on their thick sweaters and buttoned up their jackets. Finally, all three were ready and, a few minutes before nine o'clock, they set off.

Immediately, they knew that something was up. They had heard noises while they were still indoors, but had been too busy to take much notice. Anyway, there was always something going on in the harbour. This, however, was different.

The fire alarms shrieked. Then along the road raced the *Patricia*, the city's new motorized fire engine, horn blaring, firemen clinging to the side. This modern chemical fire engine was very special, and other cities had nothing like it. The old ones had not been given names. The boys ran as fast as possible, keeping the *Patricia* in sight. They could see and smell smoke, and could certainly hear a loud roaring noise, but buildings blocked their view of what was causing it. When they reached the gap that lay between the Graving Dock and the Sugar Refinery, they got their first sight of the harbour. James had a glimpse of a big ship with BELGIAN RELIEF on her side. Now they ran in single file, Alan, whose legs were shorter, bringing up the rear.

They were passing the Protestant Orphanage with its high stone wall, when, abruptly, all sound stopped.

Millicent Upham

Archie Upham

Ellen, Archie and Millicent Upham were not going to school that day. Their grandfather had died and his funeral was to be in the afternoon. They were to go to their uncle and aunt's house on Longard Road, where their grandfather had lived. Archie was unhappy about his grandfather, but was looking forward to seeing his cousin, Reg Rasley. They did not see each other every day, because Reg attended Bloomfield School, on the corner of Robie and Almon Street. He was eight, just a little older than Archie, and they enjoyed playing together. Of course, Reg did not go to school that morning either because of his grandfather's death. He and his sisters quietly looked at books, while their mother prepared for the people who would come to the house in the afternoon. They were all quiet and sad, as they missed their grandfather.

The Upham house, on Rector Street, was not far from Richmond School. Very few houses had been built there, and it was like living in the country. They could look over fields to Bedford Basin. Mr Upham had been on the night shift and had walked home up Rector Street from the railway yard earlier that morning.

Mrs Upham had a big breakfast ready, because her husband was always hungry after working all night. After he finished eating he stoked up the furnace and the kitchen stove from the huge winter supply of coal in the cellar. Leaving his wife and the three smallest children in the nice warm kitchen, he went upstairs, where Millicent and Archie were playing in one of the bedrooms. "Don't make too much noise," he told them, "I'm going to sleep." With that, he went into his bedroom, put on his nightshirt, got into bed and pulled the blankets right over his head to keep out the light. He was soon fast asleep.

A soldier at York Redoubt, more than four kilometres away, took this picture of the smoke from the explosion.

Millicent laid out the dolls' teaset that she loved. It was pure white and very dainty. On top of the chest of

drawers nearby lay her piggybank. She was saving all her pennies for Christmas. Millicent was good at saving while Archie always spent whatever he was given. He took a book from the shelf and opened it up to read. That would be quiet. There seemed to be a commotion coming from further up the harbour. "Daddy will be angry about all that noise," Millicent said.

"He'll never hear it," laughed Archie. "He always pulls the blankets right up over his head. You can't even see his nose. I don't know how he breathes." They sat on the bed, Archie with his back to the window and Millicent facing it.

Other Richmond children were at home too. Bill Swindells, who lived almost opposite Noble Driscoll, was gathering his things together for school. He and his mother were alone in the back of the house, where the windows faced away from the harbour. Mr Swindells and the other members of the family had already left for the day. Mrs Swindells was very busy, clearing up the breakfast things and putting the house in order. Bill knew that there was a fire in the harbour and was hurrying to get ready for school. He thought that if he rushed, he would have time to stop and look at the fire on his way. With his bag on his back, he headed for the door. His mother came out of the kitchen to see that he had everything. "Don't waste your time going to see that fire," she warned him. "Go straight to school." Bill opened the door.

At St Joseph's Roman Catholic School, the girls were inside. Prayers began promptly at nine. Evelyn Johnson had left home early, well before the ships had collided in the harbour below. Her piano lesson at the convent began at half past eight and she liked to be there in plenty of time. She played especially well that morning and the sister who taught music was very pleased with her. "You must have practised hard this week, Evelyn," she said. "Good for you." Now, still flushed from the praise, she ran as fast as she could to the cloakroom at the school nearby, to hang up her coat before class. One of her friends stood inside, eagerly looking out of the window. "Come and see the fire!" she called out. Billowing, black smoke towered in a column, but they could not see where it came from. Evelyn turned away. She knew she really must not be too late.

On the day of the explosion the girls of St. Joseph's would have been wearing their "tires" or white pinafores.

Dorothy Swetnam

Dorothy Swetnam curled up in an armchair in the living room of the Methodist manse on East Young Street. Her mother sat at the piano. Beside her stood Carmen, who was just about to practise his solo for the mission concert. Carmen had a lovely singing voice and, luckily, had not caught Dorothy's whooping cough. He would be out of quarantine in time for the concert. Mr Swetnam stood, leaning against the door jamb to listen.

Mr Huggins, the principal, had arrived in the train with his daughter Merle, and they were walking up from the station towards Richmond School. He knew there was a fire in the harbour, but he liked to be in school half an hour before the children arrived. He was hurrying along, when he met the father of one of his cadets. They both stopped to talk. "You run along, Merle," said Mr Huggins. "I'll catch up." Merle was quite pleased to do that. She could meet her friends and have a game in the yard before school.

"That's quite a fire down there," Mr Huggins said. "I hope those students of mine are not getting too close and making nuisances of themselves."

At the same time, the *Patricia* reached Pier 6, where the *Mont Blanc* had drifted and was now touching the end of the wharf. The timbers of the pier were beginning to smoulder. All at once the whole of Richmond became engulfed in a strange, ominous silence.

The fire had reached the barrels of high explosives in

the holds of the *Mont Blanc*. With a force that shattered buildings all over Richmond, and across the harbour in north Dartmouth, the *Mont Blanc* blew up. It filled the sky with its fragments of steel, fiery soot and oil. Mixed with harbour water, displaced by the force of the explosion, they rained down all around. The shock was felt 434 kilometres away. Windows in Truro, more than eighty kilometres from the explosion, were broken. Part of a gun hurtled through the air and landed five and a half kilometres distance, by Albro Lake beyond Dartmouth. A piece of the anchor stock, weighing 516 kilograms, was embedded in the ground at Armdale, beside the North-West Arm, just outside Halifax.

Those who were close to the explosion heard nothing. Mr Huggins was dashed to the ground. For a time he remained unconscious. When he came to, he could not hear, as his eardrums had been badly affected. He felt pain in his limbs. He thought to himself, "I am glad that Merle went on." He did not know that this terrible thing had wrecked his school and killed his daughter.

# Chapter 4

# Explosion!

Barbara Orr stood rooted to the ground by the sight and the heat of the huge fire raging below her, until suddenly she felt herself moving in a strange way, almost as if she were dreaming. A great wind seemed to have swept her up off the ground and she was rising and falling in its current, turning as she went. Up she would soar, then down into a deep black hole, then up again. Presently, the wind stopped and she was on solid earth but not in Mulgrave Park. She had landed over half a kilometre away, near the top of Fort Needham.

For a time Barbara lay still, only half conscious. Then a sharp pain in her foot and ankle brought her round. She felt with her fingers where the pain was, and then sat up in surprise to have a closer look. One of her knee-high, tightly laced boots was gone. It must have crushed her leg as it was drawn off by the suction of the explosion blast. She got up, but quickly sank down again. Her ankle could not bear her weight. She thought if she waited a while that perhaps she could gather her strength. She had to try to go home. Around her were several people, staggering, injured, all coated in black, oily grime. Barbara heard someone cry, "The Germans are here! The Germans are here!"

"It's not the Germans," she tried to tell them. She wanted to let them know that the burning ship must have blown up, but the words would not come out loudly enough.

Barbara started, sometimes walking, sometimes crawling, in the direction of her own home. After she

*Facing page:* A wall of smoke and flame where Barbara's home had been.

*Inset:* The *Imo* ended up on the Dartmouth shore although it was in mid-harbour when the *Mont Blanc* exploded.

Barbara Orr

had gone a little way, she stopped. There was no point in going any further. Down there, where her home had been, was a wall of smoke and flame. The wooden houses were ablaze. She turned to the left, away from the fires. Her aunt and uncle lived not too far away, over on Gottingen Street. She would try to reach their house. It might be better there.

On she struggled, stopping now and then to wipe her eyes. Sharp cuts stung her face and arms. She was wet and very dirty.

Finally, she reached the house on Gottingen Street. The windows were all gone, the ceilings were down, and there was a lot of other damage, but at least it was not on fire. Her Aunt Edna and two cousins, Gladys and Bill, were outside.

The old fire engine on Gottingen Street. The *Patricia* was now a wreck, and only one of her crew left alive.

"Who are you?" asked her aunt, looking at the strange figure.

"It's me, Barbara," she cried, shocked that her aunt could possibly fail to recognize her.

"You can't be Barbara," exclaimed her aunt. "Barbara has red hair." Barbara's hair, and indeed all of her, was completely blackened by the fallout from the explosion.

Mrs Orr was very worried. Her husband had gone to the Richmond Printing Works, where he was a partner with Barbara's father, and he had not returned. "Where are your mother and the other children?" she asked Barbara as calmly as she could.

"They are all gone," Barbara answered. Somehow she knew that was true.

Poor Mrs Orr hardly knew what to do. Neither of her children was seriously injured, but the house was in such a state, with shattered glass, fallen beams and plaster, that she could not even find a coat to wrap around Barbara or clean cloths to cover her cuts.

"Come along," she finally said. "We'll go to Mrs Moir's. It may not be so bad there." With her aunt's help, Barbara managed to struggle a bit further. It seemed to take hours for the little party to reach its destination.

They found Mrs Moir standing in her doorway, looking about her at the damaged houses. "Come in," she said, when she saw Mrs Orr. "Isn't this dreadful." She heard their story and could think of nothing she could say to give comfort to Barbara, but she took her into the kitchen to try to clean her up a little. The dirt was embedded in Barbara's skin and the cuts hurt too much to be rubbed hard, so it was impossible to make much improvement. Barbara looked round the kitchen. Something white and sticky covered the walls and the ceiling. Mrs Moir explained that she had been making bread that morning and had put the dough in pans to rise. It certainly had risen, but not in the way she expected.

Mrs Moir gave Barbara a cup of hot tea and then put her in a bed and covered her with a blanket. Barbara lay still, thinking about the dreadful explosion and about her family. She felt alone and helpless.

Noble Driscoll

Noble recognized the remains of Richmond School.

Noble Driscoll also heard nothing when the ship blew up. He too was lifted by the force of the blast and lost consciousness. When he first came to, he thought he was dreaming. He remembered the smoke and flames but now here he was, alone. There was haze all around, with what looked like a full moon in the distance. He got up and shook himself properly awake. A pile of shingles and rubble surrounded him, but he did not seem to be hurt. His coat and cap were gone, not a sleeve, not a scrap left. Was he the only one left alive? How would he manage? What would he eat? Noble liked to eat, and that problem struck him immediately.

Somehow he had been carried as far as Duffus Street, just behind Richmond School. He recognized the remains of the building. He began to walk down towards the water and saw a man. Good, he thought. That meant he was not all alone. He could even identify the man, a workman on the school extension. "Was it the Germans?" the man asked.

"I don't know," Noble answered shortly and kept walking. He had to find his home and make sure his family was alive. When he got there, he saw that all the windows, doors and some of the walls were gone. It looked deserted. He went on further.

Suddenly Noble saw Bill Swindells. Blood was oozing from Bill's neck, all mixed with black soot, and his clothes were in a terrible state. Even so, Noble found the sight of him reassuring. Here was someone he knew who was still alive. It suggested there might be others. He and Bill talked briefly.

"I saw your brother, Lou," Bill said. "Look, here he comes now." Noble thought Bill had made a mistake. That wasn't Lou at all but an unrecognizable, filthy creature, whose face was black as coal. Then the creature smiled. It was Lou, all right! Those big, buck teeth, shining through the soot, were unmistakable.

The two brothers walked back towards home, leaving Bill standing forlornly outside his ruined house. His mother was there, trying to pick up a few belongings. Her face was badly cut.

Noble and Lou went around to the back of the house this time. There, in the shelter of the only standing wall, were their mother and father and three brothers and sisters, clustered round the kitchen stove, that, miraculously, was not badly damaged. Soon, the other members of the family began to arrive. Only Noble's little brother, Gordon, was missing. They were still hopeful that he might be safe with some of his school friends.

The Pattison boys saw homes looking like piles of kindling wood.

The Pattison boys were running along, eager to get as close as possible to the source of all the excitement, when, in a breath, everything seemed to stop. James' next impression was that he was lying in water with big cables holding him down. He could see only a short distance because of the thick fog. After a struggle, he managed to free himself. He realized that he had been caught in the wires of the trolley line that ran along Barrington Street. Luckily, they were not live.

James pushed himself up on to his knees but collapsed again, hitting his face on the ground. Finally he struggled dizzily to his feet. His nose was bleeding and

James Pattison couldn't believe that even the tall Sugar Refinery building was a pile of wreckage.

a shingle nail stuck out of one hand. He pulled it out, and now his hand was bleeding too. A high pile of stones blocked his way, but he scrambled over it. Not far away, beyond the collapsed wall of the orphanage recreation field, he saw the body of a boy. The boy looked as if he had fallen down a chimney. Then he moved and something gleamed on his wrist. James recognized the silver watch with its shield like the spokes of a wheel. No one else had a watch like that. It was Gordon, his own brother. He was alive!

James Pattison

When the boys managed to take stock of themselves, they found that both had lost their jackets. James' schoolbag was gone too, and so was one of Gordon's boots. Although both boys were bleeding and sore, neither was seriously hurt and they were able to walk.

They searched around among the rubble, but could find no sign of Alan, their little brother. Gradually the fog lifted and the sun shone through. The whole world had changed. No buildings were standing. Even the tall Sugar Refinery was a pile of wreckage. They wondered if their father had been able to get out in time. Fires had already broken out in places, and it was impossible to tell where the streets had been. They searched some more for Alan, but with no luck. Perhaps he had gone home, they thought. They walked back in the general direction that he might have taken. James noticed a house that looked like a beaver dam. On top was a man tearing at the broken beams.

Then some soldiers came along. "Get away from here," one ordered. "The magazine in Wellington Barracks might go up next. Go up to open ground, up that way. You'll be safer." Numbly, they obeyed him. James knew that the magazine held explosives and, if it caught fire, the destruction would be even more appalling. The boys walked up the hill as far as Gottingen Street and the North Common, Gordon limping because of his bare foot. People were milling around, all worried about another explosion. Someone gave James a coat and a stocking hat, and eventually Gordon found another boot lying on the ground. It fitted not too badly. He wondered what had happened to its owner.

James Pattison lived one block away from the foundry on North Barrington Street. It was now in ruins.

Other Richmond children who had been inside their own homes, where they should have been safe, had narrow escapes when the explosion wrecked the area. Millicent and Archie Upham had just settled down quietly in the upstairs bedroom when what seemed like a huge rushing wind tore through their house, smashing the windows. The glass pierced Millicent's face and the back of Archie's head. Almost immediately their father ran into the room, barefoot and wearing his nightshirt. He wasted no time, but ushered the children out to the hallway. The stairs were gone and the oilcloth that had covered them dangled free. With its help, Mr Upham managed to reach the ground floor. He stretched out the oilcloth to make it as as rigid as possible and persuaded both children to slide down to join him. Beams were collapsing on all sides of them. They could see the harbour now because a wall had completely caved in. Their father hustled them outside. Live coals from the stove and furnace were scattered among the splintered wood of the collapsed walls, and the house was on fire. As soon as he thought the children were far enough away to be safe, Mr Upham seated them on a fallen door and told them to stay there. His feet were bleeding from the broken glass on the ground.

He ran back to the house to try to find his wife and the three younger children but the fire was now roaring. Try as he might, he could not get back into the house.

Millicent Upham

Archie Upham

He heard no sounds from inside. His boots and trousers were lying where they must have fallen from the bedroom. They were the only things he was able to rescue. He put them on. Finally, he gave up his efforts and went back to Millicent and Archie. Just as he reached the children, another railway worker came by. When he saw the state Millicent was in, he took off his own coat and wrapped it around her.

Millicent's face was cut and she had lost her left eye. Archie's wounds were on the back of his head, so they were less visible. Carrying Millicent piggyback and holding Archie by the hand, Mr Upham walked up the hill away from the harbour. Frightening sights of damage and injury met their eyes as they struggled through debris and made detours round fallen buildings. At last they reached the Rasleys' house on Longard Road, where they had planned to meet for the funeral later that day. The house was damaged, like all the others in the area, but, unlike the ones closer to the harbour, they were not on fire.

The Rasleys were with other families on open ground opposite the house. Soldiers had ordered them to go there when they toured the city to warn everyone of a possible second explosion. One of Archie's cousins, a little girl, was seriously injured and the other, about the same age as Millicent, had bad cuts on her face. Mr and Mrs Rasley were worried because Reg, Archie's friend, had disappeared.

Like the Uphams, the Swetnam family was at home that morning and suspected nothing wrong. Mr and Mrs Swetnam and Dorothy were in their living room, waiting to hear Carmen's song. The first notes were scarcely out of Carmen's mouth, when there was a tremendous crash. The roof fell in a cloud of plaster, and part of the floor gave way. The piano toppled on top of Carmen. Both he and his mother lay still. Dorothy was pinned under pieces of wood and plaster, unable to move. For a time Mr Swetnam knew nothing. Then he came to himself and looked about him. He found his wife and then his son but could do nothing for either of them. They were beyond help. Suddenly he heard Dorothy's voice, "Where are you, Daddy?" That gave him strength.

*Inset:* Remains of a shattered building.

*Bottom:* Dorothy Swetnam lived near this house, left standing on Kaye Street.

Dorothy Swetnam

He managed to reach her and made a great effort to heave off the timbers that held her, but they were stuck fast. Everything was in disorder. Then he spotted his saw. He grabbed it and started sawing through the big beams that pinned Dorothy. That hurt her, and she began to cry. He almost gave up. The furnace had been overturned, and by now, flames were coming close.

A neighbour, Ethel Bond, who came in with her sister, Bertha, described the scene a few days later in a letter: "Dorothy was in a sort of triangle made by the east wall falling up the hill, and she was so penned in her head could not get out through the hole." The plaster dust and smoke caught in her throat, and she had a violent fit of coughing. Mr Swetnam had laid down his saw. He was afraid that if they tried to pry up the wall, a beam might fall and crush Dorothy. By then, the back of the house was on fire, and they were desperate. He sawed again with all his might and managed to make a slight opening.

"Bid (Bertha) put all her weight on a piece of wood sticking out and, between the three of us, we pulled the child out," wrote Ethel. "Nothing could be done for those in the ruins as the fire drove everyone away."

Bertha rushed back to her own house, which was not yet burning quite so fiercely, and managed to grab some clothes for Dorothy and her father. Strangely dressed, they all headed up the hill away from the fires.

Other Richmond children, like Evelyn Johnson, were in school buildings that were usually considered sturdy and strong. Evelyn, who had just turned away from the cloakroom window at St Joseph's School, heard a loud roaring noise, felt sharp pains in her head and arm and then lost consciousness for a time. When she woke up, she was lying on the cloakroom floor, and the ceiling had fallen down. Other girls were nearby, some crying, not knowing what had happened.

Evelyn Johnson

Evelyn's first thought was not to find a teacher or someone in authority, but to go home. She had gone only a little way down Russell Street when she was stopped by soldiers. "Go back up to Gottingen Street and get further south, away from all this," one soldier ordered. He pointed down the hill, where the houses at the lower end of the street were blazing fiercely.

Other girls from the school came along. One of them said to Evelyn, "Your arm looks as if it's hanging off." For the first time, Evelyn examined it properly. Sure enough, it did seem to be bleeding a lot. There were now many people around and soldiers were already taking charge. Rescue must be at hand, she thought.

# Chapter 5

# Refuge

In a surprisingly short time after the explosion, soldiers, soon helped by sailors from the ships in the harbour, began rescue work. Soldiers in Wellington Barracks quickly put out the fire near the magazine, ending the fear of a second explosion. The people who had been ordered out into open spaces were thankful to be allowed to go home. Streets were soon crowded with wagons, trucks, cars, and every available kind of vehicle carrying the injured to hospitals. The city hospitals could not cope with a fraction of the number of injured but the military hospitals helped out. They were quickly filled too.

Barbara Orr lay in bed for a time, but sat up, relieved to have her thoughts interrupted, when Mrs Moir came into the room. "They are taking people to hospital, dear," she said, "and we think that you should be seen by a doctor as soon as possible." Barbara was feeling too weak and confused to make any decisions. She let herself be carried outside without saying anything, but she recognized the name "Boutilier" on the side of the wagon that stood there. It was the one that delivered fish to her house. Mrs Moir was close to tears as she watched Barbara being loaded on to the makeshift ambulance.

There were other people lying beside Barbara, some still and quiet, others moaning. With difficulty, they made their way through the streets, their progress slowed by debris. People walked wherever there was a

Sailors helping the wounded.

*Facing page:* In a surprisingly short time, soldiers and sailors from ships in the harbour arrived to help with rescue work.

clear path, many in strange bits and pieces of clothing, some showing signs of injuries.

Finally they reached Camp Hill Hospital, the big military hospital, which was scarcely finished. There Barbara was unloaded on to a stretcher, carried inside by two soldiers and left in a corridor near the entrance. For a time she lay in a group of still, blackened bodies until an orderly came by. She called out. Startled, he came over. "I thought they were all beyond hope," he said. "I'll be back in a minute." He returned with a helper, and Barbara was carried into a long ward filled with beds, where her leg was washed and bandaged. No one had time to clean the rest of her. Doctors and nurses were doing only what was absolutely necessary in order to treat as many of the injured as possible. Barbara lay in her narrow bed, wondering what would happen to her next.

Camp Hill Hospital where Barbara, Bill and Evelyn spent the night after the explosion.

Bill Swindells and his mother had been taken to Camp Hill Hospital too, but Barbara did not know that. Just after the Driscoll boys had left Bill outside his house, a group of soldiers arrived. They examined the cuts at the back of Bill's head and the deep one in his neck. His mother, hearing voices, came out of the house. Her face looked as if it had received the full blast of a window.

Bill Swindells

"Is there any flour in the house safe to use?" one of the soldiers asked. After checking the kitchen and finding that the bin had not split open, he carefully daubed flour on their cuts. It looked very strange, the thick white coating on top of the black, but it helped to stop the bleeding. The soldiers then loaded Bill and his mother on to a wagon, and they spent that night at Camp Hill.

Evelyn Johnson spent the night at Camp Hill too. As she walked along Gottingen Street, with her arm still bleeding, an army truck came by and stopped. One of the soldiers jumped down when he saw Evelyn. "You had better come with us," he said, and lifted her on to the truck. That evening, her mother found her at the hospital. Although Mrs Johnson's side was badly bruised, and she was obviously in pain, she had not taken the time to be treated. She had spent the whole day searching the shelters and hospitals for her children. She was overjoyed to find Evelyn, but still had not found her older son, Jerry. She knew though, that he had been picked up and taken to some hospital. The doctors were very worried about Evelyn's arm but said that they would try to save it.

Noble Driscoll stayed with his family around the stove in the backyard. His older brother, Cliff, went off to try to find Gordon and see what he could learn. After a time he came back. He had no news of his brother but plenty about what had happened and a suggestion for them to consider.

Just before the explosion, Cliff told his anxious listeners, a passenger train had been approaching Halifax. Vincent Coleman, the dispatcher at Richmond Yard and a man that they all knew well, was told by a sailor that the burning ship, now very close to his office, was loaded with munitions and that he was in great danger. Instead of saving himself, Coleman stayed there to send a message and stop the train. That message was, "Munition ship on fire. Making for Pier 6. Goodbye." Vince Coleman died at his post, but he stopped the passenger train, thereby saving many lives.

The train stopped in Rockingham, where its passengers got off. Now it was being loaded with injured and homeless people. Many were railway workers' families, like the Driscolls. "Come on," said Cliff to his family at the end of his story. "There's room for you too."

With Mrs Driscoll carrying five-year-old Art, who had been injured, the family set off for Rockingham. Mr Driscoll had a bandage over one eye that was filled with shards of glass. By the time they were all settled into a compartment, the younger children were hungry. Mrs Driscoll remembered that she had baked two Christmas cakes and put them in tins with tight lids. They might be safe to eat, she thought. Cliff ran back to the house, found them and took them to the train. Noble was very glad of a piece or two.

Early that afternoon, the train set off with its very unusual load of passengers. Art lay on his mother's knee, barely conscious. Doctors on the train treated the wounded passengers and, eventually, the train reached Truro.

Josephine Bishop, a young teacher in Truro, wrote to her mother next day, telling her what happened. "School had just assembled," she wrote. "I was reading

The Driscolls were among the survivors taken to Truro on this train.

the Bible when two awful explosions shook our building with great force. We thought the Germans had opened fire on Halifax. By ten o'clock, trains began to leave Truro with doctors, nurses, firemen, and fire apparatus. At noon came the call for food for the stricken inhabitants, and, at half past three, the wounded began to arrive."

The people of Truro responded to the call for help, and many waited at the station to offer their homes to those who needed shelter. Josephine Bishop was there to give what help she could. "So many little children injured," she wrote, "and their parents gone." The injured, like Mr and Mrs Driscoll and Art were taken to the courthouse that had been made ready as a hospital.

Noble and Al were told that they could go to a home at the experimental farm. They liked the idea, but first Noble had to find a washroom. The soot, oil and rich Christmas cake did not mix well, and he was very sick.

It was a long ride by horse and cart to the farm in the dark, and the boys could not see their surroundings. When they reached the house they were given a meal and had a hard scrub in a good, hot bath. They were pleased to find that the house was well supplied with hot water that gushed from the taps, as not every home had hot running water. The two boys soon sank into a big, double bed, between nice, clean sheets. They were too exhausted even to talk very much before falling asleep.

Noble Driscoll's house was on Barrington Street, not far from the house on the right.

For the first time since the explosion, James and Gordon Pattison stopped wandering and stayed on the Commons until people started to move away. Where could they go? Then Gordon suggested that they head for Central Wharf down from Citadel Hill. A Sugar Refinery boat always made a trip between there and the Dartmouth and Halifax refineries. It could take them to their grandfather's house in Dartmouth. It was a long walk to Central Wharf. Very tired by now, they stood around, waiting for the *Ragus*, as the boat was called. Finally, a Marine and Fisheries boat came. Its captain did not tell the boys that the *Ragus* had sunk off the Richmond shore, but he invited them to board his boat. He took them to Dartmouth, but his dock was quite a distance from their grandfather's house. A man on the dock ordered them very gruffly to move off. The boys did not realize just how terrible they looked.

It was almost evening when James and Gordon reached their destination. When their grandmother opened the door, she could hardly believe her eyes. The boys may have looked bad to the official on the dock but to their grandmother they were a most welcome sight. Their dirt did not matter to her. She gathered them into her arms and hugged them. The boys had hoped that the rest of their family would be there already. Their hopes were dashed when they were told that their grandfather and uncles had gone to Halifax to try to find all of them. The windows in their grand-

James Pattison and his brother saw strange sights as they walked through the streets.

parents' house had been smashed. Luckily, however, the storm windows were in the basement where they had been protected from the blast. They had been quickly installed. James and Gordon were cleaned up as much as possible, given something to eat and drink and sent to bed. Although they were worn out, they were so worried about their mother, father, brother, and sister that they could not fall asleep. Their grandfather returned and hurried upstairs to see his grandsons. They sat up eagerly when he came in, but he had to tell them that there was no news of their family.

arlier in the day, Dorothy Swetnam and her father
were making their way through the streets in their
borrowed clothes. Mr Swetnam held fast to his little
girl's hand and, when she began to cough, he picked
her up and carried her until the spasm stopped. He was
determined to get Dorothy to a safe, warm place, as far
away from the fires as possible. On they trudged to the
ferry terminal, almost at the centre of the city.

The ferry had been in the middle of the harbour
when the explosion took place. Although it had been
hurled about and damaged, it never stopped running.
Backwards and forwards it went all that day, taking

Rockhead Prison, where
Archie Upham stayed.

some people away from the wreckage and bringing others to search among the ruins.

Thankfully, Mr Swetnam helped his daughter on board the ferry. As they crossed the harbour they could see that the damage in north Dartmouth was terrible too, but fortunately far fewer people lived there. In Dartmouth, they made their way to the home of Mr Swetnam's friends, who welcomed them warmly. The windows on the harbour side of the house had been broken, but the back bedrooms were all right. Dorothy had a bath and some hot soup. Soon, she was tucked into a warm, clean bed.

From where Millicent and Archie Upham sat with their father, on the open ground above Longard Road, they could see the fires caused by the explosion raging down below. The cotton factory, nearby on Robie Street, was a mass of flames. As it was a good distance from the harbour, they guessed that its furnace must have overturned.

As soon as they heard that the danger of a second explosion had passed, Mr Upham took Millicent to Cogswell Street Military Hospital. Wounded soldiers there had given up their beds for explosion victims, who seemed in worse shape than they were.

Archie was taken to a different kind of safe haven. At the end of Gottingen Street near Bedford Basin was the city prison, Rockhead. There, prisoners were employed in the prison market garden and in breaking rocks to

Children picking up
supplies at a relief depot.

make gravel and stone chips for roads. Fortunately, no dangerous criminals were there, since most of the inmates had taken the opportunity to escape during the confusion following the explosion. The prison, a strong, stone building, was not seriously damaged. By late afternoon, George Grant, the governor, had filled the cells with people who had lost their homes.

Archie Upham was taken to the prison and found his aunt and some of her family already there. Reg, his cousin and playmate, had still not been found. Two of Reg's sisters had been taken to hospital. One, like Millicent, had lost an eye, and the youngest was very badly hurt. Mrs Rasley, even though she was very worried about her own children, immediately began to try to make Archie cleaner and more comfortable. Under the dirt, she discovered that he had a bad wound on the back of his head. It had bled a great deal, but no one had noticed, as his head was so black. Archie was given clothes belonging to one of the governor's boys. They were too big for him but were clean and in one piece.

eg Rasley, who had been missing all day, was very frightened by the sudden blast and the damage to his house. At the time of the explosion, he had been in the storeroom off the kitchen where the jars of preserves were kept. A piece of heavy, hot metal crashed right through the roof not far from him and smashed a chair. As far as Reg knew, it could have been a shell from a German ship. He expected German soldiers to come rushing in at any moment, with their guns firing. When the jars fell and shattered on the stone floor behind him, he ran out of the house without thinking, and kept going.

Reg Rasley

Not too far away, he met one of Governor Grant's sons. "Come home with me," the boy said, and Reg went. As they arrived, some of the Grant boys were leaving to visit Tower Road to check on their aunt, Mrs Grant, who ran a bakery there. Reg went with them. It was a long walk. By the time they reached Tower Road he was hardly able to put one foot in front of the other. Mrs Grant questioned him about his family, but he could not tell her much. She immediately sent someone to try to find Reg's mother and tell her that he was safe. Then she put him to bed and he fell asleep, thankful to be with caring people. He was not afraid any more.

ORR, Barbara, Kenny and Albert Sts.,
    Camp Hill.
*ORR*, William, Kenny and Albert Sts.,
    Camp Hill.

Merle Huggins, aged 11 years, who was at Richmond school at the time of the catastrophe is missing. The little girl girl is the daughter of Principal Huggins who will be deeply grateful for any information regarding her.

# Chapter 6

# What Next?

All next day Barbara Orr lay in her bed, feeling lonely and abandoned as she watched people come into her ward. She could see through a window that it was snowing heavily. As the people entered, they would shake snow from their coats. Many wore an odd assortment of clothes that did not fit very well. Probably they had lost everything and had just put on whatever they were given, Barbara thought. They would look at every patient, and, now and then, she would hear excited voices when a family member was found. She watched the scene going on around her anxiously, praying for the sight of a familiar face. Finally, it grew dark, and still the snowstorm continued. The number of people grew less. Her tears were very near the surface, but she gulped them back and tried to sleep.

Next day, there was another stream of people. Just when Barbara had almost given up, she saw someone she knew. It was her other aunt, her mother's sister, from Dartmouth. She had read Barbara's name on a list in the newspaper. Reporters were going around to all the hospitals and shelters, finding out the names of those who had been hurriedly taken there. This was of great help to people who were searching for their relatives.

Mrs Orr, Barbara's Halifax aunt, had found shelter for her family in the home of some friends, as her Gottingen Street house was too badly damaged to return there. Then, knowing that Barbara was safe, she spent every spare minute trying to find her husband.

*Facing page:* From the train window, the Swindells could see the devastation and the *Imo* beached on the Dartmouth shore.

*Insets:* Notices in the newspapers helped people locate their missing relatives.

Barbara's aunt was peering at every bed. Barbara called out, and she came over but did not open her arms to give Barbara a much needed hug. "I'm Barbara, Barbara Orr," the girl said almost desperately. The woman looked at her carefully. "Oh, you can't be," she said doubtfully, just as Barbara's other aunt had done. "Barbara has bright red hair." Barbara's face and hair still had not regained their normal colour. Once convinced, however, her aunt, who had almost given up hope, was overjoyed. Soon Barbara was able to leave

Barbara could see the heavy snowfall from the hospital window.

the hospital and go home with her aunt to Dartmouth.

Those days alone in the hospital had made Barbara even more sure that she had lost her family. Again and again she had gone over in her mind what had happened. She had pictured that terrible scene when she looked down at her old home. No one could have survived that fire. As well, by a strange instinct that she could not understand, she knew she was the only one left alive. Barbara's feeling about her family proved correct. Her father, mother, three brothers and two sisters had all

been killed in the explosion. Their home had burned down. One of her uncles had died at the printing works, which was completely destroyed. The huge concrete blocks had tumbled like toy building blocks. Most of the employees had been killed, but, amazingly, her grandfather had escaped unharmed. Her Uncle William was saved, but injured, as he had been outside, watching the fire. He was taken on board a ship in the harbour and then to Camp Hill Hospital, but Barbara had not been aware that he was nearby. His wife finally located him the day after Barbara was found. She read his name on a list in a newspaper.

Until well after Christmas, Barbara lived in Dartmouth with her uncle and aunt. Then the time came when she had to choose which family she would like to live with permanently. Both of her uncles offered her a home. Her uncle and aunt in Dartmouth had no children, and Barbara had been used to a large family. It was a difficult choice, but Barbara decided to live with her Uncle William, her father's brother, his wife and their two children, Gladys and Bill. They had lived on Gottingen Street, near her old home, and they had spent a great deal of time together before the explosion. Although it took a long time for her to adjust, eventually they became like a new family to her. Of her old life, there was practically nothing left. Her home, furniture, clothes, photographs, and the people who had meant most to her were all gone.

Some children had to remain in the hospital for several weeks.

On the morning of December 7, James and Gordon Pattison woke up at their grandparents' house in Dartmouth. By the time they had finished breakfast, snow had begun to fall. This did not stop their grandfather and uncle from leaving to take the ferry to Halifax to try to find the rest of the family. By night, the snow blocked the streets, and held up the wagons, cars and trucks that were trying to take the injured or homeless to hospitals or shelters, or to deliver food and fuel to people so that they could stay in their homes. Horses and wagons managed the steep hills and deep

James books were returned
to him sooty and damp.

snow better than motorized vehicles. Many of them had to be left where they became stuck.

Towards evening the boys' grandfather returned with one piece of good news. Their mother was safe! She had been rescued by an American sailor and was now in a temporary hospital in the Y.M.C.A. building. Every morning, their uncle would rush out and buy a copy of all the newspapers, hoping to read that the others had been found. Their grandfather had put a notice in every paper but, after a few days, their hopes were dashed. Alan and Catherine were found but had been killed, and there was no hope that anyone could still be rescued from the pile of wreckage that had been the Sugar Refinery.

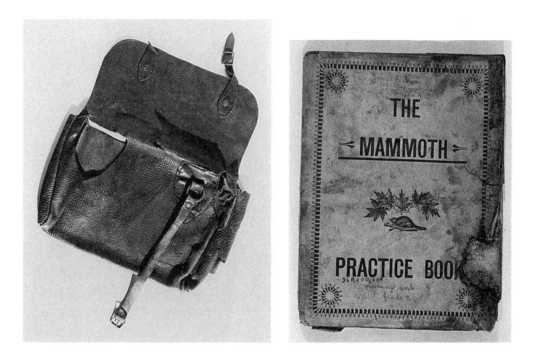

James Pattison's schoolbag and books probably saved his life.

James' schoolbag was picked up in the grounds of the ruined orphanage and returned to him, one strap missing and the leather ripped. The books were damp and sooty but they were all packed tightly together and could still be read. Perhaps the thick wad had saved James' life.

After ten days in hospital, the boys' mother joined them in Dartmouth. When the Sugar Refinery ruins were cleared more than three months later and their father's body found, James was given his watch back. The glass was gone, and so were the hands, but they had left their imprint on the face of the watch. It had stopped at ten past nine. He had always kept it a few minutes fast. That watch and the bag of books were to remain among James' most precious possessions.

No matter how often it was washed, Mr Upham's nightshirt never got clean.

Dorothy Swetnam and her father were also in Dartmouth. Although they stayed there, Mr Swetnam was hardly ever in the house. His church, Kaye Street Methodist, had been destroyed along with the manse. Three other churches were in ruins too, Grove Presbyterian, St Joseph's Roman Catholic and St Mark's Anglican. Many of the people who had attended them were killed, injured or had lost their homes. Like Mr Swetnam, their ministers were all working hard to help their parishioners.

After a few days, Millicent Upham was moved to a hospital set up in St Mary's College by American doctors and nurses who were now in Halifax. A train had left Boston on the evening of the explosion, bringing people and supplies. Other trains and ships arrived in the days that followed. Goods worth many thousands of dollars came from New England.

There was nothing that could be done to replace Millicent's lost eye, but the cuts on her face needed many stitches and the eye socket had to be treated. She was in hospital for several weeks till well after Christmas. During that time, she wore the little gold ring her mother had given her the Christmas before and refused to let anyone take it off, even though one of the doctors thought it was getting a bit tight. When Archie and his father visited her, Mr Upham asked an American doctor to look at Archie's head. The doctor removed more than twenty pieces of glass and later put in a flat piece of metal for protection.

Millicent's fragile little dishes were unbroken, but her pennies were fused together. Later, she wore her ring on a chain.

It was confirmed that Mrs Upham and the three young ones had died in their home. The rest of the family went to live with the children's uncle and aunt, until they could decide what was best to do. As soon as he could, Mr Upham went through the ruins of his old home himself. He did not want strangers to do it. Lying among that pile of rubble and ashes, he found some of the dishes belonging to Millicent's tea set. Those fragile little pieces of china had survived when everything else, the chairs, the beds, the heavy furniture, even the people, had perished. Mr Upham also found the contents of Millicent's piggybank. The pennies had been fused together by the heat of the fire. Millicent never did spend them.

Reg Rasley, Archie and Millicent's cousin, stayed on at Tower Road all winter while his father tried to fix up their house and see to the rest of the family. His sister, Annie, like Millicent, had lost one eye, and both girls were in the same hospital. They spent a lot of time talking to each other and sharing visitors. In January, Reg's other sister died from the injuries she had received.

The large supplies of clothing and furniture sent to Halifax from Massachusetts were arranged in what looked like a big store, so that people could have some choice. Reg was taken there. Not only was he fitted with clothes and boots for the winter but he also came away with a lovely sled. Like most other children in the city, he did not have school.

There was plenty of choice at the Massachusetts Relief depot.

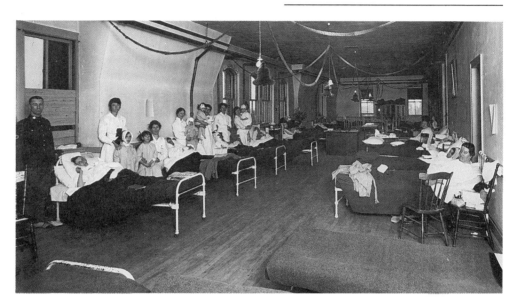

Evelyn Johnson was moved from Camp Hill Hospital to the Y.M.C.A. temporary hospital. Her uncle came to visit her. "It's too bad about your father," he said. When Evelyn obviously did not understand, he quickly began to tell her about one of her friends. Then her mother arrived, and Evelyn saw that she was dressed entirely in black. Suddenly she understood what her uncle had meant. She began to cry, as her mother explained that her father had been killed.

Evelyn was in hospital for several weeks, and her brother even longer. During that time her mother and other brother stayed with some cousins. When Evelyn could forget her sadness, she was really quite happy in hospital and grew fond of her American doctor, who made jokes and even acted as Santa Claus at Christmas. Everyone worked hard to make sure that the children who had gone through so many bad experiences should have as happy a Christmas as possible.

Many children spent Christmas in the hospital.

The morning after the explosion, Al and Noble Driscoll woke up to a new world. They were in the country in the outskirts of Truro, and the fields and trees outside their window were white with snow. Noble got up to have a better look. Al was surprised to see that the bed clothes where Noble had been lying were filthy. "Nob," Al shouted, "I thought I told you to get properly clean last night!"

"I did," Noble protested, turning from the window. He was shocked when he saw the stains he had made. Then Al sat up. "Just look at your own side," Noble said to his brother. It was just as bad. The black stayed on their skin for some time. Sheets and pillow cases were dirty each morning no matter how often the boys bathed.

After a week Al and Noble came back into Truro to be with the rest of the family. Their mother, thinking it might improve their looks, gave them a dollar to go and have a haircut. When the barber began cutting, Noble winced. The man took a better look. Little glass splinters were still embedded here and there. "You must be from Halifax," he said quietly. Then he asked about what had happened to them. He and his assistant shampooed, rinsed, removed splinters and snipped, until the boys were much more comfortable and looked a lot better.

Although it felt wonderful, both boys were very worried. How was one dollar going to pay for all this

special treatment? The barbers finished and Al, very embarrassed, offered the dollar. The owner of the shop laughed and shook his head. "You come with me," he said and led them across the street to a store, where he bought them each a complete outfit of new clothes. They did not know how to thank him properly for his kindness, especially as he must also have lost a lot of business by spending so much time with them.

By Christmas the Driscolls were settled into a big house in South Uniacke. Their father had lost one eye, and it took months for Art to learn to talk again.

The snow helped to soften the ruins of Richmond.

*Right and Below:* North
Street Railway Station,
before and after the
explosion.

Gordon was never found. But the family was together again, and that helped them to get over their losses. A baby girl was born in 1919.

After Bill Swindells and his mother had spent a night in Camp Hill Hospital, they were told that they were going to be taken to another hospital, which would not be quite so crowded. They were driven to the Rockingham train station just outside Halifax. The main station in the city, North Street, had been so badly damaged that it could not be used. A train was waiting, and they set off for New Glasgow. As they travelled round Bedford Basin, they looked back at the ruins of Richmond. The people in the train stared in silence, shocked by what they saw, even though the snow helped by blanketing the devastation.

When the train reached New Glasgow, everything was ready. The Swindells were taken to the new high school, now set up as an emergency hospital. After a time there, they moved to the home of a family who were complete strangers to them. These people might have been friends, they were so kind and thoughtful. At first, Bill and his mother had to have their cuts dressed every day. As they healed, the scars left were dark blue. Early in March, the Swindells returned to Halifax, where a new home was waiting for them.

# Chapter 7

# A New Life Begins

Something had to be done for the thousands of people in Halifax and Dartmouth who were without homes or possessions, many injured for life, women left without husbands and children without parents.

A great deal of help had already come pouring in. As soon as reports of the disaster spread, doctors and nurses arrived, as well as medical supplies, food, clothing, trucks, horses, building materials, workmen, and all sorts of supplies that would help people who had lost nearly everything. Money was sent from all over the world. Early in 1918, the Halifax Relief Commission was established by the Canadian government, which also gave a large sum of money. The Commission's role was to provide more permanent care for the people who had suffered in the explosion and to help rebuild the damaged areas of the cities of Halifax and Dartmouth.

This commission lasted until 1976, that is, for fifty-eight years. Widows, orphans and those who had very serious permanent injuries, such as the loss of eyes or an arm or leg, were awarded pensions or given a lump sum of money to try to make up for their suffering. People whose homes and possessions had been destroyed or badly damaged could also make a claim for what they had lost. Some claims were paid in full, but most were reduced.

In the middle of March, 1918, the first temporary homes were built by the Relief Commission on the

*Facing page:* Children took part in activities at the Community House on the Exhibition Grounds.

Exhibition Grounds off Young Street, after the wreck-age was cleared away. Fine, big buildings that had been used for different exhibitions were too badly damaged to be worth repairing. The Poultry and Pet Stock Show had been due to begin in December, 1917, and the advertisement told people that they could do their Christmas shopping at the stalls and booths there. Of course, that event never took place.

The new apartments were called the Governor McCall Apartments, to honour the governor of Massachusetts because his state had sent so much help.

Bill Swindells and his family moved into one of these

New temporary housing was built where the Exhibition buildings used to stand.

apartments, on Maine Avenue, when he and his mother returned from New Glasgow. Bill was perfectly happy there. He knew many of the other boys and enjoyed the sports on the new playing field. Eventually classes and games were organized. It was different from his life before the explosion, when most of his friends had been from school or church. Now that the schools and churches were destroyed, people in the temporary apartments were thrown together. They had all suffered from the same disaster and so they quickly got to know one another. After living in other people's houses for so long, the Swindells and their neighbours were de-

Teams of horses were brought from Montreal in 1918 to clear up the debris of the houses, stores, schools, churches and industries that were once part of Richmond.

Destroyed by the explosion Dec 6th 1917

House consisting of seven rooms situated at
75 Cabot St Halifax N.S.

| | | $ |
|---|---|---|
| House Valued at, completely wrecked | | 3.000.00 |
| Barn Outhouses & fencing | | 550.00 |
| Parlor | 1 Parlor suite destroyed by snow & rain | 35.00 |
| | 1 Parlor Brusells carpet destroyed | 27.50 |
| | 9 Pictures | 12.00 |
| | Photos vases & parlor ornaments | 10.00 |
| Bedrooms | 1 Comode broken | 5.00 |
| | 1 Bedstead broken | 5.00 |
| | 2 mattresses destroyed | 10.00 |
| | 2 chamber sets broken | 8.00 |
| | Pillows bedclothes etc. | 4.00 |
| Hall & stairway | Carpet & linoleum | 20.00 |
| | 3 Pictures | 4.00 |
| | Hall stove pipe | 5.00 |
| Dining Room | 1 Dining table wallnut broken | 40.00 |
| | 1 room stove | 6.50 |
| | 6 chairs | 7.50 |
| | Linoleum | 13.75 |
| | Dishes | 11.00 |
| Kitchen & Pantry | Groceries & Preserves | 12.00 |
| | Kitchen oil cloth | 14.00 |
| | Cooking utensils destroyed | 8.00 |
| Cellar | Vegetables Frozen Beets 1 Bushell | .60 |
| | Potatoes 20 bushel | 25.00 |
| | Turnips 6 | 2.70 |
| | Carrots 1½ | 1.00 |
| | Cabbage 4 Dozen | 2.50 |
| | Blinds & curtain 11 Windows | 3,642.05 |

I am willing to take oath that the above losses $ 3,463.95
are correct. to the best of my ability    Arthur E Simmons
Now living at 130 Bonvain Road      75 Cabot St

lighted to have homes to themselves.

The Relief Commission built more temporary homes of the same kind in other open spaces. The houses had wooden frames and were covered with tarpaper but they were well enough heated, and everyone knew that they would not have to live there for ever. Evelyn Johnson and her family rented one of the apartments on the South Commons, on Chatham Avenue. It was an upper flat with two bedrooms. They had been given new furniture by the Massachusetts Relief Committee and Evelyn was very pleased with it. Her new bed had a fancy brass headboard and there was a comfortable rocking chair in the living room where her mother always sat to do her knitting.

The first new, permanent homes built by the Relief Commission were ready in the spring of 1919. Two years later, they were all were finished. Evelyn Johnson

*Facing page:* Families were allowed to claim money to replace their lost possessions.

Children were happy to have a playground near their temporary housing.

Twenty rows of relief housing, called The Hydrostone, sprang up bewteen Isleville and Gottingen Streets. Fort Needham was just across from some of them.

and her family then moved into a corner apartment on Columbus Place. There were only four in the block. It was lovely to look out at the trees and not have so many people all around. Fort Needham was just across Gottingen Street, and Evelyn did not have too far to go to school. There was a little garden at the back, with a gate that opened on to an alleyway for delivery trucks. The power poles and lines were there too, so that the nice open spaces in front, with the grass and flowers,

were not spoilt.

Evelyn really liked the way the houses looked, most of all. They were built of light grey blocks made with a special kind of concrete called hydrostone. They were so thick that hardly any noise could be heard through them. The roofs sloped steeply, and all the snow just ran off. Evelyn thought that the houses looked interesting and almost a bit foreign, certainly not like the old, flat-roofed wooden house where she used to live.

Soon, everyone was using the name of the building blocks for the district, and it became known as the Hydrostone. The Driscolls eventually moved into one of the largest of the houses. Bill Swindells lived on the same street, in another new house, though not a hydrostone one. Buildings were springing up all over the area. It looked very different by 1921.

The Rasleys' house was repaired enough by late spring for the family to move back. For a time, Mr and Mrs Crowdis and their two children lived with them too. Mr Crowdis was minister at Grove Presbyterian Church and, like Mr Swetnam, had lost both his home and his church. He, too, was so busy looking after his congregation that he hardly had time to look for another house.

The Pattisons did not move back to Halifax. James and his mother stayed on in Dartmouth with James' grandparents, and James attended Hawthorne School. He did not find the work especially hard nor the other

Children play in the sunshine on the equipment given by the Rotary Club of Halifax.

students unfriendly, but he could not settle in happily. Gordon, who had been very badly upset by the tragedy that had struck his family, went away to visit an uncle in Granville Ferry for several months. It was hard for them to adjust to being such a small family now. Mrs Pattison was seldom cheerful and happy, the way she had been before the explosion.

Archie Upham and his father settled again on Rector Street in a new house. Millicent stayed on with her aunt and uncle. She was happy with them. Her aunt was like

Younger children in the temporary housing attended a kindergarten set up expecially for them.

a second mother and Millicent grew to love her.

Dorothy Swetnam and her father remained in the Halifax area for nearly two years. By that time his congregation was more settled and the new church almost ready. Mr Swetnam wanted to go and live somewhere else, away from all the unhappy memories, so he became minister in a church in Truro. Later, he remarried, and Dorothy became part of a new family.

Barbara Orr moved with her aunt and uncle to Truro, where they lived until their house could be repaired, or a new house found. The three children went to school in Truro for a few months and then moved back to Halifax to a different house on Windsor Street. They needed more room as Mrs Orr's mother and father were living with them too. That made seven people.

Barbara grew very fond of her new family, although she really missed her old life, especially at night, when she would dream that she was back again on Kenny Street with her mother and father and her brothers and sisters. The dreams became less vivid however, as time passed.

The people of Grove Presbyterian and Kaye Street Methodist churches shared a temporary church until the spring of 1920. They named it "the Tarpaper Church" as it had been built quickly of plywood and tarpaper. In 1920, a new church was ready. Called first the Kaye-Grove Church and then the United Memorial Church, it took the place of both of the others.

The largest bell in the carillon—given by Barbara Orr in memory of her family.

The Orrs, the Driscolls, the Uphams, the Rasleys, and the Swindells all attended the United Memorial Church. Sometimes Mrs Pattison, with James and Gordon, came over from Dartmouth to attend a service. In the church tower hung a carillon of bells, given by Barbara Orr in memory of her whole family. On the largest bell was engraved:

In Memoriam.
Samuel Orr, Jr. and his wife
Annie S. Orr. And their children
Ian Mary Archie Isabel & James
who departed this life
Dec. 6TH, 1917
Presented by their daughter Barbara
1920.

When the church was formally dedicated in April, 1921, Barbara played a hymn on the bells. She was nervous as she pulled the big, heavy levers that controlled each bell. "Suppose I make a mistake," she said anxiously to her cousin. "It will be heard as far away as Dartmouth." But she did not strike a false note, and the bells sounded tunefully across the area that had been destroyed by the explosion. Now that it was being rebuilt, there were fewer empty spaces and new houses stood on the slopes. The people were taking up a new life.

# Chapter 8

# Back to School

T he winter of 1918 was a very severe one, with lots of
snow and ice. This made life difficult for people
whose houses had been damaged and were no longer
weatherproof. But for Reg Rasley, who still lived on
Tower Road with his temporary family, life was not too
hard. He had a new sled and, with all the good slopes
round about, he spent many carefree hours coasting
down the hills. He really did not miss school at all.

Every morning Noble Driscoll and his sister walked
a kilometre distance along the railway line to the one-
room village school at Etter's Settlement, near South
Uniacke. They carried their lunch as well as their books.
Because Noble was one of the older pupils and always
among the first to arrive, he soon took on duties, such
as having a good fire burning in the wood stove by the
time the other students arrived. Even so, the classroom
was seldom warm. Noble could not help comparing the
country school with the old school in Halifax. The
teacher was kind and patient with Noble but both she
and the other students sometimes grew tired of Noble's
often repeated comment, "In Halifax, we didn't do it
like that."

It took some time for the schools to get back to
normal. Most teachers were busy working on one of the
committees that had been started to deal with the
effects of the explosion. School buildings were used for
special purposes. Chebucto Road School became the
official mortuary. Hundreds of people went there to
search for the bodies of their relatives. Between 1,600

and 2,000 people had been killed. The exact number was never worked out.

Both the Halifax Ladies' College on Pleasant Street and St Mary's College, a boys' school on Windsor Street, had been converted to hospitals. Morris Street School was still being used for the injured as late as July, 1918. More than 2,500 injured had been rushed to hospital on the day of the explosion, and there were just not enough hospital beds in the city. The Alexander McKay School was taken over by the Reconstruction

During the snowy winter of 1918, sleds were very useful.

Committee until an extra annex was put up in the schoolyard. Because the buildings were used in so many different ways, they needed work before they could be used as schools again.

All the schools in Richmond had been damaged. Even those that were furthest from where the explosion took place at least had broken windows. This meant a long holiday for the Richmond children. Richmond and St Joseph's Schools had to be rebuilt. Of the three buildings that made up Bloomfield School, the junior

school, where Reg Rasley had gone, was too badly damaged to fix, and the high school needed a great deal of repair. The manual training school was the least damaged and was ready for use in late February, 1918. It was shared by students from all three parts of the school.

It was May before the Richmond children began school, and even then, they attended only part time. Being back at school was very different from the way it had been before the explosion. The Richmond School students went for half a day to Alexander McKay, but many of their classmates were not there. Some had been killed, others had moved away. Almost everyone had signs of injuries and many had spent time in hospital. Scars were tinged with dark blue from the fallout of the explosion. The colour never went away.

The old problems of spreading infection became worse because many classrooms were crowded, stuffy and badly ventilated until repairs or a new building were completed. The students always seemed to have colds and, when flu broke out, the attendance was worse than ever. Eventually each school was supplied with a disinfectant soap and, something unheard of before, paper towels. Students no longer had to be sent home because they had dirty hands or faces!

All of the Richmond students had experienced great danger, and most of them had lost close relatives or friends. They now lived in different homes, with different

The new Richmond School.

The Halifax Ladies' College was used as a temporary hospital after the explosion.

furniture. Little was familiar to them any more. They even had to make new schoolfriends. It was not easy for many of them to forget what had happened and accept the changes. Some children refused to talk about the explosion, while others liked to exchange stories about their adventures.

When Noble Driscoll returned to Halifax from South Uniacke in 1919, he attended the part-time classes at Alexander McKay School. Mr Huggins was again the teacher, but most days he was so busy with other things that the class scarcely saw him. He had been unable to teach for nearly a year after the explosion, and never completely recovered from his injuries. One day, he told Noble to come and see him at the end of class. Noble wondered what he had done wrong. "You would be better off getting a job," Mr Huggins said. "I hardly have time to teach, and you are not learning anything new." Noble talked over Mr Huggins' suggestion with his father and soon left school to work as a delivery boy for Creighton's store. He drove a horse and wagon just as his brother Al had done. The old building had been completely destroyed and some of the family and workers killed, but a new store had been built.

The girls from St Joseph's School also had half-time classes, sharing the Alexander McKay School with the Richmond students and the Roman Catholic boys, whose school it really was. Evelyn Johnson had half days free and tried to keep up with her music.

*Inset:* Mr Huggins

Mr Huggins and his class at Alexander McKay

It was very hard for families to manage on the Relief Commission pension. Mrs Johnson received forty dollars a month, plus eight dollars each for Evelyn and her younger brother. Half of her widow's pension was spent on rent for their Hydrostone apartment. After she bought food and clothes there was little left for extras. At Christmas Evelyn was in a concert at school and wanted new stockings. She knew that her mother could not afford them but mentioned them to her, just in case. "All the other girls will have them," Mrs Johnson said. "I don't want you to be without." She sent Evelyn to a store that often had bargains. "Say you will be back to pay for them when the pension cheque comes in," her mother told her. Evelyn was pleased with her stockings but also felt guilty, because she know how difficult things were for her mother.

On May 20, 1918, two portable school buildings on the open space at the Exhibition Grounds were ready for use. Children of all ages and religions who lived in the Governor McCall Apartments started school there. The new school helped families from different schools and churches get to know one another.

Millicent Upham and Annie Rasley had both lost one eye and needed hospital treatment before they were able to attend school. In the autumn of 1919, a new class called the Special Class for Sight Saving, began at Tower Road School. It was for children who did not have normal vision. Both girls went there. There was no homework, because some of the homes were not well lighted. The classroom was always especially bright. School work was done orally, and the students chanted things like multiplication tables, the names of Canadian rivers, kings and queens of Great Britain, or spelling rules like " i before e except after c." For most children going to the special class meant travelling by street car rather than walking to school, but their skills improved more quickly there.

In that same year, there was a bad outbreak of smallpox. More houses than ever before were placarded with a big SMALLPOX sign. The large number of people living close together in the temporary apartments, made it a very dangerous situation. The school doctor spent much of his time trying to prevent children from catching this dangerous and disfiguring disease. By the end of 1919, he had vaccinated more than 1,700 students in the city schools.

In September, 1920, the new Richmond School, at the corner of Devonshire Drive and Dartmouth Avenue, was ready for its first pupils. Both of these streets were new too. The whole area had been changed. Anyone who had known it before the explosion would hardly recognize it as the same place. Bill Swindells was not in the new school very long before he left to go to work.

Barbara (front row, centre)
and her class at the Ladies'
College.

*Inset:* Barbara Orr

St Joseph's Girls' School was also finished about the same time, and Evelyn Johnson returned there. Her younger brother attended Alexander McKay, now the Catholic Boy's School. It was just a short walk for both of them. Her older brother was now working, and his small wage was of some help to the family.

Barbara Orr and her new family had settled into their house on Windsor Street. They were no longer in the north end of the city. After discussing the various schools with Gladys' parents, the girls agreed to go to the Halifax Ladies' College on Pleasant Street, not far from the new railway station at the foot of South Street. "You are both so keen on music," Mrs Orr said, "and the Conservatory of Music is there as well."

After the first month, Gladys exclaimed to Barbara, "Did we ever make a mistake. I hate this place. Do you?"

"I do too," Barbara admitted, "but we made our own choice. We agreed to come here. We'll just have to stick it out now."

Before long they changed their minds and grew to like the school very much. Barbara was soon busy with art, singing, piano and violin lessons, as well as all the usual school subjects. When her leg injury had healed, she also became keen on sports. All this activity helped to keep her mind off the loss of her family.

James Pattison was never really happy at Hawthorne

*Inset:* Archie and Reg

Archie and Reg (second
row) at Bloomfield School
with classmates. The
teacher's dog sits in the
middle.

School in Dartmouth. He missed his friends and the companionship of his brothers and sister. Still, he studied hard and became very interested in technical drawing and mechanics.

Archie Upham did not go back to Richmond School. From the house on Kaye Street, it was just as easy to walk to Bloomfield School. The building that was opened in 1920 seemed very grand and modern. His cousin, Reg Rasley, went there as well. It was nice to be with someone he already knew.

With new homes, new schools, repairs and rebuilding, the damage gradually disappeared, and the city looked whole again.

# Chapter 9

# A Different Kind of School

Since 1873 a special kind of school had existed in Halifax. It was the Halifax School for the Blind and it was attended by students from all over the Maritime Provinces and Newfoundland. On the morning of the explosion, many Richmond children had been near a window, some even watching the burning *Mont Blanc*. Flying glass had blinded nine children, while others like Millicent Upham and Annie Rasley, had lost the sight of one eye. After these children were treated in hospital, or were old enough, they attended the Halifax School for the Blind.

Eric Davidson was only two and a half on December 6, 1917. He was sitting on his mother's lap by the window of their upper apartment on the corner of Duffus and Gottingen Street, running his toy engine backwards and forwards on the sill. Marjorie, his older sister, stood beside them. They could hear a "Whooh! Woooh!" from the harbour.

"What's that?" Marjorie asked her mother. Mrs Davidson took two knives from the table and used them to show two ships passing each other from opposite directions.

"The noises are their signal whistles," she told the children. "That is how they tell each other what they mean to do." The fire that quickly broke out did not alarm Mrs Davidson, as it seemed too far away to be dangerous.

Eric Davidson (above) attended the Halifax School for the Blind, shown on the facing page.

When the *Mont Blanc* blew up, the glass from the window flew into Mrs Davidson's neck and face and straight into Eric's eyes. The stove fell over beside Marjorie, burning her badly. Soon Mr Davidson rushed in to help his injured family out of their damaged home.

After a month in three different hospitals, Mrs Davidson, Marjorie and Eric were allowed to go to the home of another family until they could find a place to live. It was hard for Eric. At first, he could not understand why it was always dark, and he would often ask his mother to switch on the light. Because they had to move more than once, he had to get used to different houses by feeling his way around to learn the shape of a room. As soon as the temporary apartments were ready, the Davidson family went to live on the Commons. After Eric's brother was born, they moved again, this time to Cabot Place in the Hydrostone. Next came their home for many years, a bungalow on Rector Street that had been given to Eric by an aunt. By then, he had two brothers.

When Eric was seven, he went to live at the School for the Blind and his life became very different. He no longer had his mother to take care of him or his brothers and sisters for company. Now he was a boarder and slept in a long dormitory with other boys. He had to eat school food that he did not like very much. Bells marked every activity. They told him when it was time to get up, when to go to breakfast, to class, and when each lesson was over. Eric could go home for only one night a week, from Saturday to Sunday. How he looked forward to the weekend!

Sir Charles Frederick Fraser was superintendent when Eric arrived at the school. He had been knighted by the king for his wonderful work. His own blindness gave him a special understanding of his students. He travelled all over the Maritime Provinces finding and helping those without sight, and his independence gave hope and encouragement to blind children and their families.

Although at first Eric was unhappy at school, once he began to learn new skills and make new friends he became more self reliant. Before long he was enjoying most of the activities at the school. He learned the Braille alphabet, first reading words with his fingers, then whole books, and later music. His classes included oral work in arithmetic, language, history, geography and French. Every day the children sang and played music. Before long Eric joined the junior choir.

Students were taught manual skills, starting with simple handcrafts and then more complicated work. Chair caning, woodworking, broom, brush and mattress making, shoe repairing, and other crafts prepared the older boys for jobs when they left the school. Learning to use the dangerous tools needed for their work was an important part of their training. Those with musical abilities were taught piano tuning, while others enjoyed learning to care for chickens. The eggs they collected were eaten at breakfast.

There were also sports and gymnastics. Students learned to walk with greater confidence, feeling and listening for steps and obstacles. Gradually, they worked on more complicated exercises, using equipment like wallbars and vaulting horses.

When Eric had been at the school for about two years, an ex-British army officer became the new gym instructor. He believed that the boys should be made tougher. They were too soft, he said. Every morning before breakfast, they had to run round the whole block several times and then have a cold shower. Eric was thankful that this teacher did not last long. He liked skating and boating on the school pond better.

With more than 150 blind students, safety was very important. A night watchman checked the building every hour each night for signs of fire. Fire drills were often held, and those who slept on the upper floors were taught to slide down a slippery pole. It was much faster than stairs and more fun.

Discipline was strict. Each student was allotted one hundred conduct marks at the beginning of the school year. They lost marks whenever they misbehaved. Being late for a meal cost three marks and being rude to a teacher, ten. Girls and boys lost marks for talking to one another outside class. On Mondays, the scores were read aloud to the whole school at morning assembly. Those who had lost marks had to stand up, and they felt embarrassed. Sometimes students were punished for losing too many. At the end of the year, prizes for good behaviour were given to students who had the highest number of marks left.

In September of 1923, Millicent Swindells and Annie Rasley, along with other semi-sighted students, became pupils at the School for the Blind. The special class at Tower Road School had ended. Millicent was now fourteen and Annie fifteen.Both girls found it hard to adjust to being boarders when they started living at the School for the Blind. The rules, time tables and group life were not easy to get used to after the freedom of living in a family. They did not have to learn Braille unless they wanted to and were able to study all their subjects as they had before. Millicent decided to study Braille and learned to read and write it.

Girls and boys were not expected to work at the same skills. Girls did knitting, sewing, crocheting, basketry, pottery, and other craft work. The older ones learned to cook and to manage a home. They were expected to be able to entertain guests and they practised on the teachers. They began by serving tea, with bread and butter neatly arranged on a plate, at morning recess. Then they learned to make toast, tidy the room, and

Millicent learned to read
and write Braille.

HALIFAX SCHOOL FOR THE BLIND

# BRAILLE ALPHABET.

wash the dishes and the dish towels. Later they were able to set a dinner table and serve the meal. Both the blind and the partially-sighted girls carried out these tasks.

Each school year ended with closing exercises. The choirs sang, and the students performed piano pieces, dances, and gymnastics. Then came speeches and the presentation of prizes. Eric Davidson received a prize for typing, Annie Rasley for sewing and Millicent Swindells for home nursing and cooking, typing, singing, and hand and machine sewing. In 1928, she received

Eric Davidson learned to play music using braille notation.

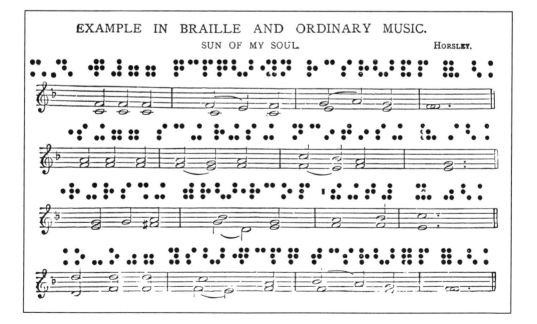

her Grade 11 certificate which included geometry, algebra, civics and ancient history in addition to the usual subjects. Millicent graduated the following year.

Students from the school occasionally went on to university. During Millicent's final year she helped two boys who had been blinded in the explosion to prepare for university. She found some of the texts she read to them boring, but she made them sound as interesting as she could. When Millicent started Grade 12 she was allowed to live at home and travel to school by streetcar. One of the teachers was ill that year, and Millicent helped to teach the younger children.

By the time he was thirteen, Eric had travelled to school and back with his mother so often that he decided to take the streetcar home by himself. The whole family waited anxiously for his arrival that Saturday afternoon. Finally, they saw him coming, beaming with pleasure. He had managed perfectly well. From then on, he was very independent. Sometimes he brought another student home with him for the night. Students in their final year were encouraged to walk around the city, take streetcars, go to concerts, visit friends and relatives, and lead a full life. Eric enjoyed playing and singing music and was interested in mechanics, especially car engines. When he left school, in 1932, Eric received his first month's pension from the Relief Commission. He used the whole fifty dollars to buy his first car.

Although Eric worked for the Canadian National Institute for the Blind, his real love was for automobiles, especially old ones. In 1944, he became an apprentice with a car repair company and qualified as a car mechanic. It was a proud day when he received his papers. He moved to Ottawa and then Toronto. Strange places were difficult for him at first but he soon managed to find his way about by streetcar. He came back to Halifax, married, and he and his wife have three children.

Eric could repair cars but, much as he wanted to, he

The boy scout troop at the School for the Blind.

Eric Davidson (centre) and
his two brothers.

was not allowed to drive one. Occasionally he found a way. On a quiet side road or along a deserted beach, with a friend at his side to help him steer, Eric managed as well as any sighted driver. "A bit to the left, Eric!" his friend would shout, as they got too near the water. "We"re heading for Ireland!" A special thrill was to venture on to the large expanse of a frozen lake, where he could produce some spectacular turns and skids.

For years, Eric worked for the City of Halifax, keeping its vehicles in running order. He lived a full life with his family, his music and antique cars, and he had a ham radio that he used to keep in touch with old friends. Many of them had been his classmates at the School for the Blind.

# Chapter 10

# Looking Back

On June 23, 1984, a reunion was held at Richmond School, and pupils who had attended the old school that was destroyed by the explosion received invitations. A special classroom had been reserved for them, with a sign on the door reading "Class of '17." Although some had not met for years, they soon began to recognize one another and were happy to have a chance to talk together.

Some came from a distance. James Pattison, who now lived in Kentville, brought his schoolbag with his grade seven books in it. All of them had been damaged when the bag was ripped from his back. His older brother, Gordon, was there too.

Noble Driscoll's home was close enough for him to walk. He arrived with his brother, Al. Noble had photographs with him, including one of his class taken in 1919 at Alexander McKay School, before the new Richmond School was finished.

Millicent (Upham) Swindells was there, with her husband, Bill, and brother, Archie Upham. Like Noble and many of the others, their homes were not far from where they had lived at the time of the explosion.

James Pattison's school books brought back long forgotten memories. "I never could stand those awful math problems with the tons, hundredweights and pounds," someone said.

People talked and laughed as they pored over the old photographs. "Did I really look like that?" asked a

James Pattison with his books and schoolbag.

*Facing page:* The Halifax Explosion Memorial Bell Tower on Fort Needham overlooks the site of the explosion.

Noble Driscoll

Reg Rasley still has the piece
of the *Mont Blanc* that
crashed through his roof
on December 6, 1917.

dignified looking lady, pointing to a little girl with a big bow in her hair and a mischievous expression.

"You certainly did," her former classmate answered with a smile, "and you were always up to something."

A touch of sadness crept in as some of the faces were recognized.

"That's Annie Campbell," said a woman, pointing to a happy looking little girl in a class group. "She was killed."

"Isn't that one of the Orrs?" asked someone else.

Before he retired in 1924, Mr Huggins had arranged a ceremony in memory of the eighty-four Richmond School children who had been killed in the explosion, including his own daughter, Merle. A bronze plaque, recording the names, was placed on the wall in the new school. On this day, the girls and boys whose names appeared on the plaque were sadly remembered by their old friends. Soon, however, the conversation became cheerful, as the "Class of '17" talked of the things that had happened to them since they were at school together.

James Pattison had taken courses in drafting and mechanics and eventually became foreman of the mechanical department at the Dartmouth Oil Refinery. He had spent several interesting years in Peru. Noble Driscoll was employed by the Nova Scotia Liquor Commission and had managed the store on Agricola Street for many years. Archie Upham, like his father, worked on the railway. Millicent had trained as a hairdresser in Montreal before settling in Halifax and marrying Bill Swindells, who had become a baker. His fruitcakes were famous. Reg Rasley, now retired, had been a printer. Although James Pattison had moved to Kentville, the others lived within walking distance of where their homes had been at the time of the explosion.

"What do you think was the cause of the explosion? Who was to blame?" someone asked. These questions lead to a lively discussion.

One man said his father had always been convinced that it was sabotage, a German plot. Many people believed at the time that there could have been a spy on the *Imo*. The captain and the pilot had both been killed, they said, and that was suspicious too. Less than a week after the explosion, an enquiry was begun in Halifax with judges, lawyers and more than fifty witnesses. Many shocking facts came out, including evidence that the harbour was not being well run. The enquiry was followed by a trial, and the judge blamed the *Mont Blanc*, because in his opinion, it had not followed the rules of navigation. The owners of the *Mont Blanc* appealed to the Supreme Court of Canada, where it was decided that both ships had been at fault. Finally, the highest court at that time, the Privy Council in London, England, gave the same verdict. Both ships were to blame.

By the time this decision was made, the people were too busy rebuilding their lives and their city to be

Millicent and William Swindells

Archie Upham

concerned. Most of them said that, had it not been for the terrible war, the explosion would never have happened. After talking it over in Richmond School sixty-seven years later, the class of '17 agreed.

The following year, explosion survivors met together on another special occasion. The chimes of the carillon of bells in the United Memorial Church had marked all sorts of ceremonies over the years. They had often been played by Barbara Orr and sometimes by Eric Davidson. As time went on, the weight and vibration of the heavy bells had caused the tower to crack, and the carillon had

Barbara (Orr) Thompson stands beside the carillon just before its removal.

The bells are removed from the lawn of the United Memorial Church.

to be taken down. For eight years it lay covered in tarpaulins, on the church lawn. Then, in 1983, the Halifax Explosion Memorial Bells Committee began plans and fund raising to build a new tower to house the bells. On June 9, 1985, that tower was dedicated. Standing on top of Fort Needham, it overlooks the site of the explosion and the area that used to be Richmond.

Millicent Swindells and her grand-daughter, Anne-Louise Ihasz, inserted a time capsule in the tower, to be opened on December 6, 2017, the hundredth anniversary of the explosion. It is hoped that Anne-Louise will be there to open the capsule with its 1917 and 1985 aritfacts.

Eric Davidson

At their dedication, the bells in their new tower were played by Barbara Orr, now Barbara Thompson, with the help of her cousin, Bill Orr. Unlike the first time she played them, she did not have to pull heavy levers. A keyboard inside the tower is linked electrically to the bells. As she played, Barbara could not help but remember that winter day, sixty-eight years earlier, when she had landed very near the spot on which the tower now stood.

Many of the survivors gathered around the tower to hear the bells. Millicent and Bill Swindells, Archie Upham, Reg Rasley, Noble Driscoll and his two older brothers chatted together in the sunshine. Eric Davidson, with his wife and sister, Marjorie, were not far away.

Evelyn Johnson, now Lawrence, could not be there

Evelyn (Johnson) Lawrence

Dorothy Swetnam-Hare

because she was not well enough, but she read the reports in the Halifax newspaper where she had worked for many years. Dorothy Swetnam-Hare, who had become a professional pianist and piano teacher, lived too far away, in Calgary, to come.

As the bells rang out, the large crowd became silent. For Barbara, Noble, Bill, Millicent, Archie, Reg, Eric, and others, it was mere chance that they were standing on Fort Needham in the sunshine. Only a moment's good luck on that winter's morning many years ago, allowed them to be here as survivors of the Halifax Explosion of December 6, 1917.